Real Estate is HOT
Fundraising is NOT

5 Keys to Revolutionize
How Charities & Champions Fund Their Causes,
Careers, Companies, & Communities

Cami C.E. Baker

**TRANSFORM
PUBLISHING**

Real Estate is HOT, Fundraising is NOT
5 Keys to Revolutionize How Charities & Champions Fund Their Causes, Careers, Companies, & Communities

ISBN: 978-1-957013-49-7
eBook ISBN: 978-1-957013-50-3
Library of Congress: 2022935809
Printed in the United States of America
First Edition

Contents

Foreword

Video/Audio #1

www.theraoc.com/book#recording1

Dr. Russell James reads his Foreword

You hold in your hand the practical playbook for real and meaningful transformation. <u>Real Estate is HOT, Fundraising is NOT</u>, is the transformation for the causes you care about, your work, and your life.

Transformation isn't about small adjustments. (Small doesn't cut it.) Transformation is about "going BIG!" Yes, it's nice when someone writes a $50 check to a worthy cause, but it's not transformational. The hard reality is that meaningful change for the important causes in your life won't come from ten dollars here or twenty there. Instead, they will come with transformational funding that gives worthy charities the resources to create meaningful change in our world.

Where does this major transformational funding come from? It comes from major gifts of assets—not from pocket change. When it comes to assets, the "500-pound gorilla" in most Americans' portfolios is not a checking account. It's not even CDs or savings bonds. It is, and always has been, one asset: real estate. That's how most Americans build real wealth. That's how most Americans hold real wealth. If we are going to create transformational change for important causes in our country, we must "go big!" *Going big* means focusing on the biggest assets...charitable gifts of real estate.

I am a numbers guy who teaches tax law and publishes research in economics journals. My research analyzes massive data sets covering hundreds of thousands of people and charities. The numbers are clear. Transformational philanthropy comes from major assets like real estate. But numbers aren't the problem. The problem is action. People can understand the idea and nod their heads at the numbers. But then...nothing. They don't act. The disease is inertia and fear. The cure? You are reading it right now. This book is the cure.

People fear charitable real estate. Charities fear it. They've heard scary stories of deals gone wrong. They have some vague notions about environmental liability. They've got grumpy CFOs who only want to work with cash. But there is good news. All these worries completely disappear just by understanding the new approaches described in this book.

But it's not just people and charities who fear charitable real estate. It's also real estate agents. They may understand real estate, but not charitable real estate. What even is charitable real estate? How does it make sense? Once again, there is good news. This book gives agents a step-by-step process to make money while making a difference in the world.

Transformation starts with understanding. This book provides exactly that. But nothing happens without action. This book shows you the "how" and will kick you in the rear. If you read this entire book *and follow its knowledge,* it can be the start of something new for you. It can be the start of something transformational. It can be the start of something BIG!

***

The REAL Agents of Change encourage you to reach out to Dr. Russell James on LinkedIn. He has an extensive list of resources, videos, books, reports, and research that he generously gives to those who ask. (Tell him we sent you!)

***

Russell James, J.D., Ph.D., CFP®
Professor of Charitable Financial Planning
Texas Tech University
www.LinkedIn.com/in/EncourageGenerosity

THIS is a REVOLUTION

You are forewarned that you cannot unlearn the TRUTH. The Truth is...Real Estate is HOT, Fundraising is NOT! No matter what city, year, or market you are in, real estate will always be a better way to fund non-profits than traditional fund-raisers. PERIOD.

Non-profits who are not growing their endowments from the proceeds of gifts of real estate are doing their organizations (those they serve) a disservice. It is irresponsible to know what you will know from this book and not take action. We are all involved in fundraising committees, Facebook groups, and conversations where these are discussion topics.

- "We need more funding!"
- "How will we feed thousands of kids/animals/ veterans with our fund-raiser being canceled?"

11

- "Our university, church, shelter, and organization are struggling. So, ask your friends to buy another raffle ticket, come to another golf tournament, and eat another overpriced cookie from our bake sale!"

To take part in these conversations as a Charity or a Champion (whether you represent a Cause, Company, or Community), once you learn what this book will teach you and then choose NOT to speak up about this knowledge, you have succumbed to the worst form of hypocrisy imaginable. Up until this very moment that you are reading this page, you have had an excuse—whether you were simply unaware that non-profits can get six times their charitable donations through gifts of real estate, or even if you have heard of real estate donations but were under the misguided impression that this way of funding would be too risky or complicated. Either way, this is a fair warning. There is NO EXCUSE once you know the truth. Ignorance has kept the causes, companies, and communities you care about stuck in "Fundraising" mode. Or what could be called "Fun draining" complaining mode.

Once you read this book, you will know the truth. You will have a moral obligation not to hoard this information if you have a conscience and truly care about causes, companies, and communities. You will know that ANY and ALL of the 1.3 million non-profits in this country have an EASY, ZERO RISK way of adding, on average, $550,000 to their bank account from ONE donation of real estate. You will learn that companies and communities who love and support these causes, cannot only STOP taking money out of their pockets, but can put money IN their pockets by serving them and leveraging the strategies in this book.

Stop reading now if you are not ready to TAKE A STAND for those you say you are here to serve. Nothing is more painful than knowing this solution for millions of people and not speaking up. Nothing is more painful unless you are the ones in the pain that we want to help relieve. The pain of the hungry, the homeless, the faithless...All those who The REAL Agents of Change are Ready, Willing, and Able to stand for!

THIS is a REVOLUTION.

Revolution:
- A forcible overthrow of a government or social order in favor of a new system
- A dramatic and wide-reaching change in the way something works or is organized or in people's ideas about it

There are 5 Keys that Revolutionize Charitable Gifts of Real Estate for Charities and Their Champions. If you are a Champion and ready to overthrow the old system in favor of a new one and change the way charities and their champions are rewarded for embracing these visionary ideas, turn the first key.

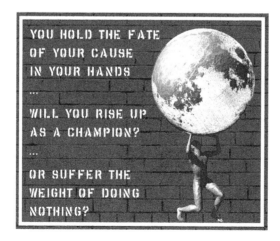

The REAL Agents of Change

Video/Audio #3 of the following Section at:
www.theraoc.com/book#recording3

Are YOU a REAL Agent of Change (RAOC)?

1

Are YOU a REAL Agent of Change (R.A.O.C.)? Are you REALLY ready to take on this moniker that has such depth and meaning? Purposeful, Passionate, and Pragmatic...yet Playful, Peaceful, and Positioned. This title gives you access to A Tribe...A Revolution...A Paradigm shift in how non-profits are FUNded! You become part of "The RAOC," as we have become known!

You are a RAOCSTAR! We encourage you to "RAOC N' ROLL" ... "RAOC Out"... and follow the "Rollin with The RAOC Tour" as our Revolution Expands Exponentially through Experiences, Explorations, and Expos all over this great nation!

The tour is led by the founder of The RAOC, yours truly, as I travel in my RV, "The Hammer," providing information, education, and certification regarding how Real Estate is creating REAL Change for non-profits by the BILLIONS! Before you join our Facebook group, get "The RAOC" tattooed on your chest, or register for the Charitable Real Estate Masterclass, you need to know what we are talking about and what this has to do with "The Legacy Listing" and being part of The RAOC Revolution!

Facebook.com/groups/therealagentsofchange

Let's look at what we mean by **"REAL Agent of Change."**

Some of Our Favorite Descriptions for "Agent of Change" and "Change Agent"

"The motto I taught my students, 'find your passion and act on it,' embodies my definition. An Agent of Change is someone who sees a problem in their community, large or small, and does something to take action for substantial change. This person listens to people in the community where the issue exists and makes sure they truly understand the root of the problem before implementing a new idea. This person is willing to take risks and doesn't always claim to know the answer. Instead, they are willing to ask challenging questions and help find creative solutions. An Agent of Change dares to think outside the box and make an impact greater than them-self."

Jennifer Coil of EducationPioneers.org

"Every organizational change, whether large or small, requires one or more Change Agent. A Change Agent is anyone who has the skill and power to stimulate, facilitate, and coordinate the change effort. Change Agents may be external or internal. The success of any change effort depends heavily on the quality and workability of the relationship between the Change Agent and key decision-makers within an organization."

Fred C. Lunenburg, Sam Houston State University

George Courol: 5 Characteristics of a Change Agent

"Working with schools and organizations, I have been fascinated with the correlation between the speed of change and the people 'leading' the charge. The schools that push boundaries of what can get accomplished seem to move a lot quicker with a larger amount of 'buy-in' through the process."

1. **Clear Vision:** A Change Agent does not have to be the person in authority, but they need to have a clear vision and communicate it clearly with others.
2. **Patient, yet Persistent:** Change does not happen overnight, and most people know that.
3. **Asks Tough Questions:** It would be easy for someone to come in and tell you how things should be, but then again, that would be someone else's solution. When the solution is someone else's, there is no accountability to see it through. When people feel an emotional connection to something, they will whole-heartedly move forward.
4. **Knowledgeable and Leads by Example:** Stephen Covey discussed the notion that leaders have "character and credibility." Leaders are not just seen as good people, but they are also knowledgeable in what they are speaking about.
5. **Strong Relationships Built on Trust:** All the above means nothing if you do not have solid relationships with the people you serve. People will not want to grow if they do not trust the person pushing the change.

The REAL Agents of Change

Video/Audio #4 of the following Section at:
www.theraoc.com/book#recording4

The Backstory of How The RAOC Came to Be

2

How The REAL Agents of Change (The RAOC) Came to Be

When I learned about Charitable Gifting of Real Estate in December 2019, I was ON FIRE to learn everything I could! I asked myself, *why have I never heard of this? How could I have accomplished the following yet had never heard of this magical unicorn that brings together my two favorite things worldwide?*

- Fifteen years of hardcore real estate experience
- 10+ years of non-profit fundraising experience
- Attended thousands of networking events coast to coast
- Exchanged tens of thousands of business cards with real estate professionals, the non-profit sector, main street USA businesspeople, and anyone else with a pulse who had a card with a bad head-shot on it

Guess what!? I'm not the only one who asks those questions. Over two years of more than full-time, DEEP DIVING, complete immersion, 10-hour days, studying, interviewing experts, being interviewed as the expert, and putting together a class to certify "Certified Charitable Real Estate Specialist (C.C.R.E.S.)," and with thousands of hours in this conversation and having met thousands of fund-raisers, board members, real estate professionals, community leaders, visionaries, and even financial advisors, I am asked the following question EVERY... SINGLE... DAY.

"If this is so great, why have I never heard of it?"

If you have the same question, don't worry, we got you covered! In this book, you will learn:

1. What Charitable Gifting of Real Estate (CGRE) is.
2. Why you may have never heard of it.
3. What a "Specialized Non-profit" is.
4. How CGRE benefits:
   a. Non-profits
   b. Realtors
   c. Financial Advisors
   d. EVERYONE ELSE
5. What the 5 Keys to Revolutionize Charitable Gifts of Real Estate are.
6. Who to talk to, What to say, and How to say it.
7. My personal favorite: How to LEVERAGE Real Estate for REAL Change. (Because knowing "What" CGRE is, is one thing, knowing what to DO with it is entirely different.)

A few months into learning about CGRE, after a LOT of intense study, research, interviewing those who were already doing it, and strategizing on how to proceed, I wasn't sure what to call this "something." I had come up with clever names for groups, including: "The Alliance," ... "Be an Ally," ... "Be in Alignment." Also, I created logos and wasted time and money trying to make something happen.

One day I was thinking about who I am and how I want to show up, and what words or titles would describe me and what I was doing—bringing charitable gifting of real estate to the world in a bigger way than it had been seen since it was added to the US tax code over 100 years ago. I was googling and came across "Agent of Change." I liked how it described how I felt about myself as an agent taking a stand for change and those I want to attract, mingle with, and do business with.

There was also a way to play with the word "agent." Since I desired to attract real estate agents, I started looking at creating a Facebook group and noticed there were several "agents of change" and variations of "Change Agents." While I am sure they all felt the same affinity I did to be a change in the world, I thought, *with what we are doing (listed below), there's plenty of room for other businesses to join us in promoting the revolution, "Make Money Making a Difference!"*

- Helping 1.3 MILLION+ non-profits in America
- Harnessing 43% of our nation's wealth held in real estate
- Having $1 BILLION+ real estate gifts donated to non-profits annually through OUR Tribe, which translates into $50 MILLION in real estate commissions and more assets under management for financial advisors

When I thought of all the children who would be saved from human trafficking, the millions of animals that would be fed and loved, the land that would be conserved, the churches and universities whose doors would remain open, and all the GOOD DEEDS from all these deeds donated for good, I thought, *I don't know about those other Agents of Change on Facebook, but WE ARE THE "REAL" Agents of Change!*

I started referring to us as "The REAL Agents of Change" with a hard emphasis on REAL, and people loved it and began referring to themselves that way! I could hear the pride in their voices when they would talk about the group. I don't know who said it first, me or my right-hand homie, Danielle (our brilliant design master that makes all our marketing pretty), but one of us said we are "The RAOC!"

It brought tears to my eyes the first time I heard someone in the group refer to us, in a matter-of-fact tone...it is what it is ...duh, that's the name...kind of way... as The RAOC. I knew we had found our name...our calling...who we are... when it was rolling off tongues effortlessly and with smiling faces.

So, I ask you again: Are YOU a REAL Agent of Change?

The REAL Agents of Change

Video/Audio #5 of the following Section at:
www.theraoc.com/book#recording5

I AM a REAL Agent of Change Declaration

3

Does the following resonate with you?

I Am a Real Agent of Change

A **REAL Agent of Change** takes a STAND for those we are called forth to serve and support.

We believe you can make excuses, or you can MAKE IT HAPPEN, but you CANNOT do both.

We are Go-Getters, Do-Gooders, Trailblazers, and Visionaries who know that Making Money and Making a Difference SHOULD go hand-in-hand.

A **REAL Agent of Change** is open to new ideas, eager to TAKE ACTION, and BOLDLY goes where others cannot even see.

We plant our flag, burn our bridge, and walk through the fire to RISE UP transformed.

We look for reasons why something WILL WORK, not why it won't.

When others ask, "Why bother?" a REAL Agent of Change's motto is: "If it is a benefit to all, including myself, then I MUST do it!"

We SERVE instead of Sell.

We COLLABORATE vs. Compete.

We understand that GIVING and RECEIVING are simultaneous.

We know the difference between a transaction and
a TRANSFORMATION.

A **REAL Agent of Change** is INFLUENTIAL and uses this
SUPERPOWER for GOOD!

We know that our ACTIONS, or lack thereof, have an
IMPACT on our family, community, marketplace, and
the world. We do not take this for granted.

We Inspire. We are Inspired. We are Inspiring.

We are an Inspiration for everyone we meet!

A **REAL Agent of Change** knows that we can DOUBLE
PROFITABILITY for ourselves and all those with whom
we partner.

We are Passionate, Purposeful, Playful, Pragmatic, Present,
and Positioned as a Partner who PROMOTES, PROMOTES,
PROMOTES the benefits of Charitable Real Estate, knowing
our Causes, Careers, Companies, and Communities deserve a
WIN-WIN-WIN!

If those statements light you on fire, then we need to talk!
We need to Communicate, Conversate, and Collaborate at the
highest level! (cami@theraoc.com)

If these truths are too much for you, that's okay. But, if you
want to learn how to leverage real estate for REAL change, this
book is still for you! Whether you are a real estate professional,
part of a non-profit, in the financial sector, a property donor, a
visionary with altruistic intentions, or looking for tax benefits,
you will get what you came here to receive.

I Am a Real Agent of Change

A REAL AGENT OF CHANGE TAKES A STAND FOR THOSE WE ARE
CALLED FORTH TO SERVE AND SUPPORT.

WE BELIEVE YOU CAN MAKE EXCUSES, OR YOU CAN MAKE IT HAPPEN,
BUT YOU CAN NOT DO BOTH.

WE ARE GO-GETTERS, DO-GOODERS, TRAILBLAZERS, AND VISIONARIES WHO KNOW THAT MAKING MONEY AND
MAKING A DIFFERENCE SHOULD GO HAND AND HAND.

A REAL AGENT OF CHANGE IS OPEN TO NEW IDEAS, EAGER TO TAKE ACTION, AND
BOLDLY GOES WHERE OTHERS CAN NOT EVEN SEE.

WE PLANT OUR FLAG, BURN OUR BRIDGE, AND WALK THROUGH THE FIRE TO
RISE UP TRANSFORMED.

WE LOOK FOR REASONS WHY SOMETHING WILL WORK, NOT WHY IT WON'T.
WHEN OTHERS ASK, "WHY BOTHER?"... A REAL AGENT OF CHANGE'S MOTTO IS:

"IF IT IS A BENEFIT TO ALL, INCLUDING MYSELF, THEN I MUST DO IT!"

WE SERVE INSTEAD OF SELL.
WE COLLABORATE VS. COMPETE.
WE UNDERSTAND THAT GIVING AND RECEIVING IS SIMULTANEOUS.
WE KNOW THE DIFFERENCE BETWEEN A TRANSACTION AND A TRANSFORMATION.

A REAL AGENT OF CHANGE IS INFLUENTIAL AND USES THIS SUPERPOWER FOR GOOD!

WE KNOW THAT OUR ACTIONS, OR LACK THEREOF, HAVE AN IMPACT ON OUR FAMILY, COMMUNITY, MARKETPLACE,
AND THE WORLD. WE DO NOT TAKE THIS FOR GRANTED.

WE INSPIRE... WE ARE INSPIRED... WE ARE INSPIRING...
WE ARE AN INSPIRATION FOR EVERYONE WE MEET!

A REAL AGENT OF CHANGE KNOWS THAT WE CAN DOUBLE PROFITABILITY
FOR OURSELVES AND ALL THOSE WHOM WE PARTNER WITH.

WE ARE PASSIONATE, PURPOSEFUL, PLAYFUL, PRAGMATIC, PRESENT AND POSITIONED AS A PARTNER WHO PROMOTES,
PROMOTES, PROMOTES THE BENEFITS OF CHARITABLE REAL ESTATE KNOWING OUR
CAUSES, CAREERS, COMPANIES, AND COMMUNITIES
DESERVE A WIN WIN WIN!!!

I Am a Real Agent of Change

The REAL Agents of Change

Video/Audio #6 of the following Section at:
www.theraoc.com/book#recording6

Is This Book For You?

4

This book is for you

...If you've ever heard the term "Make Money Making a Difference," and you thought to yourself, *Duh, isn't that what we should be doing? or I already do that! or I want to do that!*

...If you are an experienced real estate professional who loves our profession yet wants something different to reignite your fire for the business!

...If you're looking for, or didn't even know you were looking for, a truly unique way of standing out and showing up. Maybe you're already sitting on boards at non-profits, donating 10% of your commission, volunteering at fund-raisers, or leading the fundraising committee. If you would LOVE to be "The Hero" the community needs, it's for you. Or maybe you're not the "Superman" hero type, but you sure would like to see your causes get funded.

...If you could make more money while making a difference, it wouldn't hurt your feelings! It could be your *how to leave a legacy* that is top of mind for you. Being able to do that now— long before you are gone—would be even better!

...If you are a seasoned financial professional who has known for years that donating real estate to non-profits is a beautiful thing, but you've run into the problem that has kept this the "Secret Niche"...which is that 99.9% of non-profits don't, or won't, take real estate. Perhaps you have a client list of generous people you know are philanthropic and would like to "Give Smarter."

35

...If you have clients who would be super grateful to you for helping them avoid capital gains tax and collect all the other tax benefits from a charitable gift of real estate. Maybe you don't know who would donate real estate, but you sure would like to add real estate donors to your client list!

...If you have heard us talk about how you can SIGNIFICANTLY add to your assets under management and are curious how The REAL Agents of Change can make it possible.

...If you are a non-profit that realizes,

"Cash is NOT king in fundraising."
~ Dr. Russell James

View the full report at
www.theraoc.com/faqs#reports

...If you have heard the studies by Dr. Russell James that your non-profit could be bringing in SIX TIMES the endowments if only you could benefit from anything other than cash, but you don't have a clue how to make the shift. It could be that you've heard horror stories about other non-profits that have taken real estate. Still, you have also heard we have a completely RISK-FREE way for you to benefit from gifts of real estate without even knowing the property's address. Maybe you do take gifts of real estate, but only if it is debt-free, local, or easy, but you'd like to learn how to benefit from real estate anywhere in the country (or the world). Or, just maybe, you know **Real Estate is HOT...Fundraising is NOT,** and you would like to keep all your options open so you can serve the people, places, and things your mission statement was created to serve!

...If you are a visionary, forward-thinking business or community leader who supports those mentioned above. You want to be a part of the solution...a contribution to your community...a socially responsible business that knows being socially responsible isn't just the right thing to do, it is the necessary thing to do. After all, 87% of people say they will choose the company, product, or service provider whose business is on purpose and supports causes they care about. With 1.3M non-profits in the United States, instead of picking one, three, or ten to support, you are here because you see the benefit of Positioning, Partnering, and Promoting with The REAL Agents of Change who love, support, and want to fund THEM ALL!

After all...

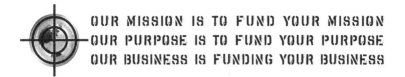

OUR MISSION IS TO FUND YOUR MISSION
OUR PURPOSE IS TO FUND YOUR PURPOSE
OUR BUSINESS IS FUNDING YOUR BUSINESS

Other authors and experts can share the nitty-gritty details and specific tax codes that can get you into the weeds regarding the charitable gifting of real estate. I have copies of books that you can spend hours, weeks, or a whole lifetime drilling down about details of tax law, donor-advised funds, and the analytical aspects of charitable gifting of real estate. However, frankly, these books just bore me to tears!

I intend with this book to keep it simple, explain the basic concept of charitable gifting of real estate, and share strategies for what to do with the knowledge once you know it. They say knowledge is power, yet...

**Knowledge becomes empowering
when it is put to good use!**

And that, my friend, is what this book is about.

This book is NOT for you

...If you only want to make money, and making a difference doesn't mean anything to you. If you are only money focused there is nothing wrong with that, yet what we are doing requires commitment and conviction to and for others. So, if doing your own thing without regard for others is your thing, this book will only irritate you.

...If you only want to make a difference, and making money is icky to you. People with hang-ups about money, thinking that money is the root of all evil, or are averse to the idea of making money while making a difference. You can simply volunteer if that is you. However, if truly making a difference is on your agenda, unless you are independently wealthy, the difference you make can be magnified 100-fold when you personally are abundant while partnering and promoting together.

...If you are hung up on old-fashioned "This is how we have always done things" or "That's too risky/complicated" or you have the scarcity mindset of "We don't know anyone who would (fill in the blank)." This concept is SO SIMPLE and way easier than any three-month planning for a fund-raiser or grant application! You just need to have an open mind, a desire to serve who you say you serve, and an eager "childlike" curiosity of... "OOOO... How can our Cause, Company, or Community benefit from these strategies!?"

...If you are looking for a "Get Rich Quick" or overnight funding of any kind. You will learn that there are people right this red-hot minute who would donate real estate through you if they only knew they could. You will learn that donors NEED tax write-offs and appreciate this option throughout the year for many reasons. You will also build the strategy muscle around how 87% of people will choose the companies and people who are "Socially Responsible," giving us the unfair advantage of having the C.C.R.E.S. designation starting on day one. All of this leads to more clients, more introductions, more cash donations, and overall, more Resources, Relationships, and Revenue for everyone involved! Just know this is a process like anything else worthwhile, and we are here to support our Champions as much as they want us to!

The REAL Agents of Change

www.the raoc.com/book#recording7

**The 5 Keys to Revolutionize
Charitable Gifts of Real Estate**

The 5 Keys to Revolutionize Charitable Gifts of Real Estate

You may have picked up this book to learn what "Charitable Gifting of Real Estate (CGRE)"is, and we will get into that in the next section. Or you may just want to know the "How" around this topic, which is fine as well. However, we invite you to start thinking about what to "Do" with this new skill you will be acquiring. Meaning, what would it look like to be "Proactive" in the quest for gifts of real estate, or shall we say, The Legacy Listing?

Be Proactive

To learn what charitable gifting of real estate is, yet not to take action to create the conversations that would attract them, is to be in a state of "Reactiveness." Ready to react if it ever happens to come up. It is this worst disservice to those you say you serve. To be "Proactive" means proactively informing others that this is an opportunity to attract The Legacy Listings that fund the causes, communities, and companies you care about.

Even though $9 BILLION a year is donated to non-profits through gifts of real estate, we meet non-profits who tell us they receive calls regularly with offers of real estate that they turn down before knowing about the right resources. It is such a new concept to 99% of people. We also hear others say: "We have never been offered real estate. If we do, we will let you know." "My clients have never asked our real estate company about giving real estate away. It's not a need we have to fill." "I don't know anyone who would donate real estate. That may work in other cities (states, neighborhoods, markets, demographics), but it won't work here."

We encourage you not to fall into this limited, scarcity mindset. The next section, Key 1, will prepare you to react when someone brings up a real estate donation. It is Key 2, Key 3, Key 4, and Key 5 that will prepare you to proactively attract and unlock the Fun, Flowing Funnel of Funding that comes from taking ACTION and having The Legacy Listings increase your Resources, Relationships, and Revenue that RAOC!

 Don't sell yourself—your company— your organization— those you care about— short by not opening to the abundance that this **"Secret Real Estate Niche that is Funding Non-profits by the BILLIONS"** can bring to your career, community, cause, culture, and all the people, pets, and places on the planet you want to improve!

After all, this is a revolution!
...The RAOC Revolution!

The REAL Agents of Change

Video/Audio #8 of the following Section at:
www.theraoc.com/book#recording8

Story of "Parable of the Pipeline"

6

Story of "Parable of the Pipeline"

This story explains the difference between a one-check fund-raiser and continuous funding from real estate.

Hundreds of years ago, there was a village far away from the water source that the villagers needed for survival. There were two young men whose job was to fetch buckets of water on demand. They "Reacted" to a need as it arose and supplied the resource (the water) when it was requested.

One day, one of the young men thought *there must be a better way to get the water to the village.* He realized he could only carry limited amounts of water with limited time. He was growing older and could see the village growing and needing more water... more water than they could provide, one bucket at a time.

So, he began to build a pipeline from the water source to the village. He knew it would take even more time to dig the trenches, lay the foundation, and get the water flowing. But he also knew that once the pipeline was in place, he could retire from the laborious task of reacting to the village's on-demand needs. Lastly, he felt responsible for the legacy he wanted to leave for himself, his children, and the village—the legacy of providing them all with more than enough water for generations to come.

He knew as the village grew, it would need more water to help the growing number of people, farms, and cattle and sustain its growth, life, and happiness. He knew that building the pipeline

was worth the extra time, effort, and energy because the water would be there for those who needed it. Just turn the tap on, and WALA! Life-giving water on demand.

In this analogy, the water is the funding. The village is a non-profit. The villagers are all whom the non-profits serve. The fund-raiser activities we have always done to bring in a one-time cash infusion have served us well. The fund-raiser is the "reaction to a need" and is the one-bucket at-a-time funding. They have kept the village alive, and the villagers sustained.

However, our villages are thirsty! The villages are experiencing a drought, they are growing, and their needs are expanding. So, to create a "Proactive Pipeline" to flow funding freely in anticipation of all the needs is just plain smart! It is a strategic use of time, talent, and treasure to create a pipeline.

Unlike a traditional fund-raiser that requires so much planning and resources in a time where the very event could be canceled or poorly attended, isn't it refreshing to know that breaking ground on this pipeline

FUNDRAISERS BRING IN ONE BUCKET AT A TIME.

simply requires some education and information to allow our donors to learn how to give smarter?

We all have been bucket carriers." I have carried many buckets. First, I carried buckets when a child needed surgery,

48

then when horses needed saving, cancer cures were being sought, and land needed conserving. Since you are reading this book, I'll bet you have carried lots of buckets, too! BIG buckets, maybe. Multiple buckets, sure. PROUD member of the "Bucket Carriers Club!" For those who love carrying buckets, we love you! Keep carrying them! After all, the villagers are thirsty, and we are not suggesting the bucket carrying stops.

For those who want to leave a legacy of pipelines to last long after we are gone, continue to the 5 Keys to Revolutionize FUNDING from Charitable Gifts of Real Estate.

The REAL Agents of Change

Video/Audio #9 of The Following Section at:
www.theraoc.com/book#recording9

Overview of The 5 Keys

7

Key #1: Learn
Learning what Charitable Gifting of Real
Estate is and

- How it works
- How it benefits everyone involved
- How this is the basic prerequisite of all we do at The REAL Agents of Change

You will learn the basics here in this book, and we encourage you to sit in on the "The RAOC Revolution, Charitable Real Estate Masterclass." You can register to be our VIP Guest in the next LIVE Charitable Real Estate Masterclass or get immediate access to the course by visiting:

www.theraoc.com/masterclass

Key #2: Lead Generate
Knowing what CGRE is, empowers you to have a new level of conversation and opens doors previously closed or simply unknown to you. So, let's discuss WHO to talk with, WHAT to say, and HOW to say it. This way, real estate donations are realized.

Key #3: List and Liquidate

The first step with 99.9% of real estate donations is to list it to liquidate it—in other words, sell it—so the non-profit world gets FUNDED!

A "Legacy Listing" is real estate donated and listed for sale to benefit the non-profit world. To liquidate means the listed real estate has been sold, allowing the proceeds to Leave a Legacy for the donor, the non-profit that receives the proceeds, and the advisors who were part of the process.

Sometimes, but rarely, the donation is managed, maintained, and used by the non-profit it is donated to. Keep in mind, these properties can be donated from anywhere globally, and the proceeds can benefit any non-profit(s) in the world. Then, just like "Hot Potato," we pass it off to a local real estate professional.

Key #4: Leverage

Even before the Legacy Listing has been listed, "Cause Marketing Campaigns" can be leveraged to build awareness, a business, and bank accounts. Leverage happens with "Positioning, Partnering, and Promoting" with others who benefit from being socially responsible. Public Relations, Marketing, and Being Seen and Heard as the "Certified Charitable Real Estate Specialist (C.C.R.E.S.)" will attract customers, consumers, and clients who, when polled, 87% say they will choose the company, product, or service that is Socially Responsible.

Non-profits, take note! You want to know business people

financially benefit when they assist you with your cause. Being socially responsible isn't just the right thing to do, it's necessary to do in business. It is better to embrace this fact and support businesses who support you, because a rising tide raises all ships.

Key #5: Leave a Legacy

Everyone involved in procuring the Legacy Listing, benefits financially, spiritually, emotionally, and mentally. Also, they can leave a legacy for themselves, their children, organization, company, community, and whatever is important to them.

When we discuss the 7 P's—from Purpose to Payoff ™ — we will explore YOUR Payoff. What kind of Influence, Impact, Income, and Inspiration do you want to be, do, and have? The great news is, charitable gifts of real estate can and will help you receive and achieve all of it!

So, without further ado, let's dive deep into Key #1!

The REAL Agents of Change

Video/Audio #10 of the following Section at:
www.theraoc.com/book#recording10

Key #1 Learn

Key #1: Learn

There are 1.3 million non-profits in the United States, and that number is growing every day. 99.9% of those non-profits, if you were to offer them a check for $500, a piece of property valued at $500,000, or cash, would take the cash. There are many reasons for that. Some non-profits have restrictive acceptance policies that don't take non-cash assets. Even those not encumbered by any restrictions don't have the staff, expertise, or resources to handle a gift of real estate. Sometimes, these donations require money to pay off mortgages, put on a roof, or manage and maintain the property while it is on the market. Few non-profits will accept real estate on a very limited basis.

- If the real estate is local to where they are
- If it is mortgage-free
- If it is a simple transaction that won't require much capital to make it happen

Yet even those transactions require approval from the board, which can take weeks or months and makes the transactions complex, inconvenient, and difficult for the donor. One of the many reasons donors give real estate when there is a simple system in place is for the convenience of the experts who can make quick decisions. Unfortunately, that is not the case for non-profits that take real estate on a limited, restricted basis.

Suffice to say, the reason thousands of Realtors have never heard of it is that 99.9% of non-profits "Can," by law, accept real estate, but don't. So even though the average donation from real estate is $550,000, no matter how beneficial it is, they simply say "No" to gifts of real estate.

- NO to the risk
- NO to the complexity and time
- NO to the responsibility and unknown outcome
- NO to another story of a real estate deal gone wrong
- NO to the "Mission Drift" (To divert manpower and attention to a real estate transaction is to divert from their mission for those they serve.)

So, the reason you've never heard of it is because if non-profits won't accept gifts of real estate, then why would real estate companies teach it? Why would financial advisors suggest it to their clients?

The second question I had, which most people ask me, is: "Are there really people giving their real estate away?"

Yes! $9 billion a year is currently being donated to non-profit organizations through CGRE. If you do the math, with an average of $550,000 per real estate donation, it equates to about 18,000 donations a year. So, yes, real estate donations are happening! I have interviewed many non-profits, Realtors, and people who are part of this whole society. I've heard them say, "We've been offered real estate for many years." For example, a gentleman from a national health-related non-profit mentioned they are offered real estate, but they were not accepting it until they had this resource.

Another group, a land conservancy, said they are offered real estate all the time. If they could "conserve" the land, that was one thing, but what about all the real estate offered that they can't? They call these "trade lands." (Real estate that can be "traded" or sold so the proceeds can go to funding their mission.) However, the ability to take on trade lands for them brings up the same issues real estate brings up for all the other 99.9% that don't take it. This conservancy was actually "Proactive" enough to look for ways to facilitate these trade lands, which is why we met.

 **People ARE donating real estate.**
Who? Why? Where do you find them? Further in this book, there's a large list of benefits for donors. However, we would like to address this right here, right now.

80/20

80% donate real estate because it is the RIGHT THING to do and because they LOVE the cause. They are altruistic. They are veterans and want to help veterans. They have a house full of animals and want to help animals. Their mother had breast cancer, and they're passionate about finding a cure.

People have "Time, Talent, and Treasure" to share with the world. You may have the time and talent, allowing you to volunteer or even run the non-profit you are passionate about. However, there are others without the time and talent to spare but who have the same passion and their treasure—real estate.

20% donate real estate because it is the right strategy for them and their situation when it comes to estate planning, avoiding capital gains tax, and having the ability to write it off their adjusted gross income (AGI). However, everyone's situation is different. We are not CPAs, attorneys, or tax consultants. We will always suggest that you seek guidance and counsel from experts who can advise you properly. However, there are many stories, case studies, and examples of property donors who didn't even have a specific non-profit in mind. In other words, it was not an act of helping humanity that brought them to the decision to donate real estate. It was a business decision.

Here are success stories representing each donor category, altruistic donations, and good business decisions.

www.theraoc.com/donations

Where do you find them?

We will get into this more in Key #2; for now, just know:

- You already know them
- You WANT to know them
- They WANT to know about CGRE and will be grateful you gave them the option

The REAL Agents of Change

Video/Audio #11 of the following Section at:
www.theraoc.com/book#recording11

Key #1 Continues, The Secret Sauce

The Secret Sauce #3

We need a Specialized Non-profit. The very small handful of specialized non-profits exists solely to accept gifts of real estate, take on all financial and environmental risks, liquidate the real estate, and give the proceeds to the non-profit that the donor wants money to go to. They make all of this happen so the donor can make the Charitable Gift to the non-profit they want to benefit.

Just as an FYI, as we get more into this topic later, here are a couple definitions we find important to clarify.

Definitions

Philanthropy: The love of mankind & humanity; generosity in all its forms; the giving of time, talent, and treasure to make life better for humankind.

501(c)3: An IRS designation for qualified organizations that provide goods and services for the public good.

Charitable Gifting of Real Estate (CGRE)

In 1917, the United States government implemented a tax code that gave property owners the ability to donate real estate (and other non-cash assets) to a legitimate 501(c)3. This benefits the non-profit and the donor.

- Non-profit has an asset they can liquidate to leverage the proceeds for their programs.

- Property Donors get two main benefits:
  - One of those benefits is not paying capital gains tax. That's right! When a piece of real estate is donated to a non-profit, no capital gains tax is paid on what is donated.
  - The other tax benefit is taking the "appraised value" as the basis for the deduction on their Adjusted Gross Income (AGI), minus any cash pulled from the value.

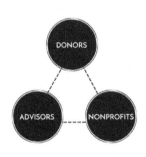

A third stakeholder in this equation is the "Advisory Community." Those who are able to advise their clients about these benefits. We like to think of it as the "Triangle of Trust." It looks like the photo to the left.

As we have already discussed, the non-profits themselves have stopped these transactions from happening. They are all legitimate reasons for not doing these deals and remain REALLY GOOD reasons for non-profits to NOT get into the real estate business! Even if they have the most experienced real estate team on their board, putting this much "Time, Talent, and Treasure" into real estate deals would be irresponsible for most non-profits. It would create "Mission Drift" and divert attention from their primary purpose. A handful of non-profits employ a full-time staff and have an actual department to handle real estate deals. However, even the largest non-profits in the US hand their real estate off to a 3rd party "Specialized Non-profit."

Specialized Non-profit Differences

The skills and services provided by the right specialized non-profit are well worth sharing the transaction's proceeds. So that is how they get paid. After all, they are a 501c(3), and so they survive on "donations" just like other non-profits.

EZ and Risk-Free for All Other Non-profits

I did the research and interviewed six specialized non-profits. I met one who keeps 100% of the proceeds from a donation! That's right! They keep it all. The donor gets the tax benefits they want, but they cannot designate their favorite non-profit to benefit. It's a brilliant marketing strategy on their part.

I met a similar specialized non-profit with a list of 6-10 non-profits they partner with that you can choose from to give a portion of your proceeds to.

I met another that keeps 70% of the proceeds from the sale of the real estate to handle the transactions! Wow, talk about working the system. You bring them real estate, and they keep the lion's share.

Lastly, I met one that keeps only 30% of the proceeds from the sale of the real estate.

Out of all the specialized non-profits I have met, two stood out above the rest; and one of them we chose to always refer first to our REAL Agents of Change.

Our Personal Favorite Specialized Non-profit
We chose them for these reasons:

- They will collaborate with any of the 1.3M qualified 501c (3)'s in this country. They will handle the whole process from start to finish and grant the proceeds to any non-profit the donor wants it to go to.
- They keep the least amount of the proceeds. They only keep 2-10%, with an average this year of 5.9% of the proceeds being kept handling the transactions. Although some specialized non-profits will also take a fee upfront, this one does not take a fee.
- They guarantee a FULL Commission to the real estate agents who list The Legacy Listing.
- They are BRILLIANT with decades of real estate and philanthropic backgrounds. They are easy to talk to and are some of the nicest people you will ever meet. You can meet them in the following videos.

Interviews:
www.theraoc.com/book#interviews

Success Stories:
www.theraoc.com/donations

The REAL Agents of Change

Video/Audio #12 of the following Section at:
www.theraoc.com/book#recording12

WIN-WIN-WIN The Benefits

10

Important Point:

The following benefits for everyone involved are benefits when leveraging The REAL Agents of Change and our vetted resources, including but not limited to the specialized non-profit.

Some of these benefits are certainly true because of charitable gifting of real estate in general. However, these donations are certainly not "Risk-Free" if the non-profit is handling it themselves. Also, there is no guarantee of a "Full Commission" if the process does not involve us. Keep these things in mind as you read through why this is a... WIN-WIN-WIN!

Non-profit Benefits

- They can receive the benefits of gifts of real estate but avoid the risk and liability.
- They can embrace their donor's best interest, allowing gifts of appreciated assets.
- They can strengthen donor relationships by tapping their wealth bucket, not their income bucket.
- They can grow their endowments at six times the rate of non-profits that only accept cash.
  (As per Dr. Russell James, Professor of Texas Tech.)
- They can receive three to seven times more from existing donors. (Jackie Franey: The Nature Conservancy)

- They can expand the number of major gifts without adding new names to existing donor lists.
- They can do all of this without a traditional formal fundraising campaign.
- They can bring in an average donation of $550,000
- They can be "Proactive" vs. "Reactive."
- They can Leverage a Legacy through The Legacy Listings.

***

Non-profits who learn how to inform donors that they can "benefit from" CGRE in working with our team don't need to change their acceptance policies because our specialized non-profit partners are the non-profits accepting the real estate.

***

Donor Benefits
- They avoid significant capital gains tax from appreciated real estate.
- They qualify for a tax deduction against adjusted gross income based on the current appraised value.
- They preserve liquid assets to protect their lifestyle.
- They can eliminate a complex asset from their estate.
- They can simplify an asset that transfers to the next generation.
- They experience convenience. "Please take

this off my hands," some of them say.

- They can receive a partial cash payment for any reason, which is called a "bargain sale." They can use this money to:
  - Pay off debt
  - Receive the return of their initial investment
  - Tailor the size of their charitable gift and tax deduction
  - Purchase replacement life insurance for their heirs
  - Take a vacation.
- They can Leave a Legacy and enjoy seeing, knowing, and participating (if they wish) in how they have made a difference through The Legacy Listing they donate.

Realtor Benefits

When partnering with The RAOC and becoming a Certified Charitable Real Estate Specialist (C.C.R.E.S.)

- They can earn a full commission, meaning "Make Money Making a Difference."
- They can switch focus to a seller who's not emotionally attached to the property
- They can elevate to advisory status
- They can be featured on the national database as a C.C.R.E.S.
- They have a Unique Sales Proposition with an untapped new niche
- They strengthen relationships with existing clients
- They are introduced and referred to high-net-worth

clients whose current Realtor isn't informed
about CGRE
- They can get Full Commission Legacy Listings from
other Realtors whose non-profit needs the funding
- They can get public relations (PR)...media coverage
- They can expand their professional and social sphere
- They can be "Proactive" vs. "Reactive"
- They can Leave a Legacy by becoming a Legacy
Listing Lister

Financial Advisor Benefits
- They can move a hard asset (real estate) into their
assets under management
- Their client can receive cash from the real estate
donation for:
  - Life Insurance
  - Purchase Stock
  - Other assets to be managed
- They can preserve the next generation of clients by
moving these assets to a Donor Advised Fund for
their heirs
- They can be featured on the national database as a
C.C.R.E.S.
- They have a Unique Sales Proposition with an
untapped new niche
- They strengthen relationships with existing clients
They are introduced and referred to high-net-worth
clients whose current financial advisor isn't informed
about how CGRE can benefit ANY non-profit

- They can get public relations (PR)...media coverage
- They can expand their professional and social sphere
- They can be "Proactive" vs. "Reactive"
- They can Leave a Legacy through The Legacy Listings

***

Businesses that Position, Partner, and Promote CGRE with those above also benefit. You'll see why when we get into the chapter on Leverage.

***

When it comes to learning about charitable gifting of real estate, the best way to do that is to sit in on the Masterclass that The RAOC has put together for you. Currently, we do it on the third Tuesday of the month. As a reader or listener of this book, you can sit in for free.

www.theraoc.com/masterclass

Other Resources Regarding CGRE

Dr. Russell James did a study and read over a million tax returns from more than 200,000 non-profits over five years. His research has proven that when non-profits accept non-cash assets, their endowments can grow by six times what they bring in with cash only.

View Full Report
www.theraoc.com/faqs#reports

RAOC Interview
www.theraoc.com/faqs#drrusselljames

Library of Q&A Videos
www.theraoc.com/book#faqs

Charitable Real Estate 101 Brief Overview
www.theraoc.com/book#101

Playlist of Interviews with The RAOC Participants and Experts of CGRE

www.theraoc.com/book#interviews

The Charitable Real Estate Masterclass. Deep Dive into CGRE The RAOC Way

www.theraoc.com/masterclass

The REAL Agents of Change

Video/Audio #13 of the following Section at:
www.theraoc.com/book#recording13

Key #2 Lead Generating

11

Key #2: Lead Generating

In my first book, Mingle to Millions: The art and science of building business relationships and mastering referrals, I discussed how I got involved in real estate. Get the first chapter for free at:

www.theraoc.com/book#m2m

My story involves alcoholism, being a single mother, and moving to a part of the country where I didn't know anyone. When I got sober, I answered an ad in the newspaper...back when newspapers were a thing. That divine intervention was a job to work for an extremely successful real estate agent who did 100+ transactions a year. I became a listing coordinator and had more experience working for him in 1 ½ years than most agents acquire in a twenty-year career. It was a blessing that gave me a significant advantage and launched me into the top 5% of real estate agents in my first year, once licensed. That book is about how to "Meet and Mingle," or what you may know as networking, but we refer to as "NetWebbing." What's the difference? Thank you for asking!

Networking is a "random activity." NetWebbing is a "planned strategy." The analogy involves the "archetypes" we meet

Net Webbing IS STRATEGIC, AND A SOPHISTICATED WAY TO SET YOUR INTENTION THROUGH YOUR MINDSET & ACTIONS, BEFORE AN EVENT.

while out "networking." The first chapter of the book describes the Skunk, Squirrel, Shark, and Spider we meet at any gathering. NetWebbing involves being the strategic and savvy spider who creates a web so all she wants comes to her... instead of hunting and chasing.

When I first learned about CGRE, I thought Mingle to Millions and NetWebbing had their day...old news. However, I have now realized that CGRE is the best form of NetWebbing ever. It is THE MOST FABULOUS icebreaker, door opener, conversation starter, and business building strategy ever!

While sitting through a conference about CGRE, I listened with an active filter. With decades of experience in real estate, NetWebbing, strategic business building, and all the events I had attended, the filter was the culmination of years of

- Knowing what it's like to be in the trenches as a Realtor
- Cold calls
- Competing for listings
- Negotiating and cutting commission
- Endless networking events
- Wanting to have a Unique Sales Proposition
- Wanting to be a contribution
- Wanting to make a difference, yet needing to

make money and not knowing how to do both simultaneously
- Meeting tens of thousands of businesspeople
- Partnering with both profits and non-profits to do "Cause Marketing" to help them all "Make Money Making a Difference"
- Knowing the struggles of fundraising
  - 3-6 months of planning
  - Committee meetings
  - Asking the same people over and over to donate cash, volunteer, buy a raffle ticket, or attend a gala, golf tournament, or car show… AND the event gets CANCELED after all that!

That day at the conference, I heard something that motivated me to learn more… "Specialized Non-profits." My first order of business was to find these specialized non-profits. I initially interviewed six and told all of them, "I don't want to bring

you one, ten, or one-hundred real estate donations. There are two million Realtors. What if we certify 1% of them to bring this information to their markets all over the country?"

One of them was most aligned with me. They said, "Tell your real estate friends we pay a FULL commission to list donations."

WHAT?!

It all started to click as to how much of a **win-win-win** this truly is for everyone involved!

Don't forget to download the first chapter of
Mingle 2 Millions for free!
www.theraoc.com/book#m2m

The REAL Agents of Change

Video/Audio #14 of the following Section at:
www.theraoc.com/book#recording14

What's Next?

12

"What's Next?"

The specialized non-profit and I got to work on creating the "Charitable Real Estate Specialist" certification class. We became great friends over the first eighteen months. They told me that everyone they have ever spoken with about CGRE loves it! No one thinks it is a bad idea. Everyone asks, "What's Next?" and "Now that we know what CGRE is, what do we do with this information?" The simple canned answer is to **TALK TO PEOPLE!** Or, as our good friend, Dr. Russell James, says, **"Share the 4 S's: Story, Story, Story, Stop talking!"**

Share the Story

- "Non-profits just like yours are bringing MILLIONS of dollars, and you can too!"
- "OH MY GOD, our board needs to have an emergency meeting! We were just talking about how we need $100,000 in funding, or our program will get shut down, and I think I found the solution!"
- "Hey Bill, you know how we were just discussing the changes in capital gains tax and the 1031 exchange? I found a way you can avoid paying capital gains tax altogether!"
- "Mary, I know you love animals and are doing all you can do to support your favorite animal shelter. I just attended a class that taught how animal shelters are funded, on average, $550,000

without a traditional fund-raiser or writing a grant! You need to hear about this!"

- "As a financial advisor, George, you're always talking about how you have such generous clients who want to do more for their communities. I have stumbled upon a tool you can provide them that other financial advisors are unaware of. There's a zoom this week you can sit in on to learn about it."
- "Teresa, there is a way to turn hard real estate assets into assets under management and get your foot in the door with high-net-worth individuals to double your managing portfolios!"

The short answer to the question, "What's Next?" is to TELL people! Invite them to a meeting we host for you. Send them to our Q&A video library. Bring them to our LIVE class or send them a link to the prerecorded class. Give them this book!

Go to www.theraoc.com/book for all these resources.

This book was created to provide information and education. To open the hearts, eyes, and minds of those who can do something powerful and empowering with the funding and friends created with this new awareness. So, reach out to us and ask how you can get physical copies of this book at half price to hand out to your donors, Realtors, financial professionals, clients, community, and all the non-profits in your marketplace that you want to do business with! <u>Real</u>

<u>Estate is Hot, Fundraising in Not</u> was designed to be an easy read, something you can leverage to "Position, Partner, and Promote" charitable gifting of real estate to fund your cause, community, and company by the multi-millions! But for now, let's get back to the strategies of what's next!

Confused People Do Nothing

This concept is SO SIMPLE, yet foreign to 99% of people. It is even foreign for the non-profits who DO take real estate, but only if it is local, mortgage-free, and easy. Tax accountants, CPAs, estate planning attorneys, and financial professionals who know that donating real estate would financially bene-fit a non-profit and their clients from a tax perspective have rarely known about a non-profit that accepts real estate. Also, they haven't heard of a 3rd party specialized non-profit that can handle the risk-free donation for everyone involved.

Even the financial professionals who know of "Advised Donor Funds (DAF)" are not leveraging real estate for REAL Change. How do we know? Because less than 2% of the funding non-profits receive comes from the 43% of real estate! So, we want to give them credit because 65% of what comes in is suggested and instigated by a financial professional. Yet, EVERY week we have financial professionals attend the Charitable Real Estate 101 Overview, and they are mind blown by what we are doing.

www.theraoc.com/101

Let's have compassion, patience, and understanding that not everyone will just "Get it." Sharing a story that gives them an opening to hear what you are saying from the perspective of "What's In It For Them" is MASSIVELY important. We encourage you to make a list of 10, 20, 50, or 100 people who need, deserve, and would be highly served to hear the story. However, let's lay some foundational groundwork before you reach out; this way, you don't blow them out of the water with too much information.

It is possible to ruin your ability to assist, quite literally, millions of people with this knowledge if your approach is more from your head than from your heart.

The REAL Agents of Change

Video/Audio #15 of the following Section at:
www.theraoc.com/book#recording15

The 7 P's from Purpose to Payoff (™)

13

The 7 P's
FROM PURPOSE TO PAYOFF (TM)

Here we will go through the 7 P's, describing each P from the first P to the last, and then reverse engineer them so you can see how interconnected they all are. You will learn

- How each P builds from the one before
- How not understanding and implementing the 7P process could leave you not knowing about a great way to fund non-profits
- How to take full commission listings
- How to add assets under management
- How to recruit teammates
- How to be seen as socially responsible
- How to save all the kids, veterans, animals,
  and environments in the world, and
  leveraging this concept to the fullest potential

Have, Do, Be vs. Be, Do, Have

There is a concept we would like you to consider as you go through the 7 P's. This concept is the difference between "Have, Do, Be" and "Be, Do, Have." We all hear people daily say things like:

- "When I **have** more time, I'll do those things to be more successful."
- "When I **have** more money, I'll buy better food quality and **be** healthier."
- "When we **have** better weather, I'll do stuff outside and **be** able to get in shape."
- "If only I could **have** more money, I'd be able to **do** more marketing for my business, and then I can be successful."
- "When the pandemic is over, I'll **have** "in-person" fund-raisers. *THEN* we will be able to raise the funds we need."
- "When I retire, I'll **have** the time, money, and ability to **do** XYZ, and then I'll be happy, healthy, and comfortable."

This mindset is around needing to have something before there is a willingness to do an action that will result in being what we want. A wise woman taught me long ago to reverse engineer this for empowerment. She said, "Cami, when you are 'being' who you want to BE, you will DO what that person would be 'doing' to HAVE what that person would 'have.' Waiting to have something is an excuse not to take action, which leads to justifying why you're not being happy, healthy, wealthy, or whatever you want."

Set Intention, Pay Attention, Create Retention

The 7 P's help us to "Be" who we want to be seen and received as by setting the intention to pay attention to what we are "Doing" so we are "Having" the retention of the Resources, Relationships, and Revenue that RAOC!

When you know how to leverage it the way we do at The RAOC, Charitable Gifting of Real Estate can provide whatever you want.

- The first 3 P's are focused on who you are *Being* and how to Set Intentions.
- The second 3 P's are focused on what you are *Doing* by Paying Attention to your actions.
- The last P is what you can *Have* by Creating Retention of Resources, Relationships, and Revenue that are all imperative for Influence, Impact, Income, and Inspiration!

Don't you just love when systems and processes come together like that!

The REAL Agents of Change

ideo/Audio #16 of the following Section at:
www.theraoc.com/book#recording16

Specialist vs. Champion

14

Specialist vs. Champion

Specialist (Head)

- A person highly skilled in a specific and restricted field
- Possessing or involving detailed knowledge or study of a restricted topic

Champion (Heart)

- A person who fights or speaks for another person or in favor of a cause
- One who battles for another's rights or honor
- A winner of first prize or first place in the competition

As we get into the 7 P's from Purpose to Payoff, I invite you to search your heart, mind, and soul regarding whether you want to be a "Charitable Real Estate Specialist" or a "Charitable Real Estate Champion."

Head

Taking our masterclass, passing the test, and paying a couple of hundred bucks will get you to the Certified Charitable Real Estate Specialist (C.C.R.E.S.) designation. In addition, you will be highly skilled and knowledgeable about this sophisticated HOT topic, giving you an unfair advantage over 99% of others in your field.

Intellectually you will have details others do not know. You will be added to our "International Database Map" and have the credentials that set you apart, along with some specialized marketing pieces.

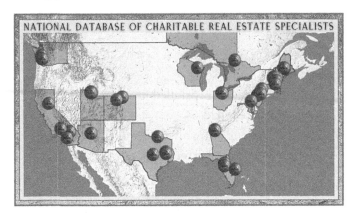

NATIONAL DATABASE OF CHARITABLE REAL ESTATE SPECIALISTS

Heart

There is another invitation here that is a massive leap from your head to your heart. An emotional, spiritual, and heart centered way to **STAND for what you believe in, be the VOICE of the voiceless, and take BOLD ACTION as The Champion!**

Being "The Champion" is not for everyone. That's why not everyone is a Champion! Being The Champion requires you to plant your flag, make a declaration, tell people the truth, and know that being part of a

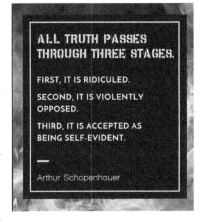

ALL TRUTH PASSES THROUGH THREE STAGES.

FIRST, IT IS RIDICULED.

SECOND, IT IS VIOLENTLY OPPOSED.

THIRD, IT IS ACCEPTED AS BEING SELF-EVIDENT.

—

Arthur Schopenhauer

paradigm shift in how things are done is not for the faint of heart. Arthur Schopenhauer summed it up best when he explained the stages of truth.

**"All truth passes through three stages.
First, it is ridiculed. Second, it is violently
opposed. Third, it is accepted as being self-evident."**

Here are prime examples of progressive innovation and society's
acceptance of the truth.

- People opposed indoor plumbing, saying it was
  unsanitary to have an outhouse in the house.
- People couldn't understand how automobiles would
  replace horses when there was grass everywhere, and
  at the time, there were no gas stations.
- People said the internet was a phase and wouldn't last.
- Blockbuster had the option of partnering with
  Netflix. Oops!
- Uber has all but removed cab companies
  from existence.
- Have strangers stay in strangers' houses?
  Whoever would allow that! Airbnb makes more
  profit with no brick and mortar to manage than
  all hotels combined.
- This is how we have ALWAYS done our
  fundraising.

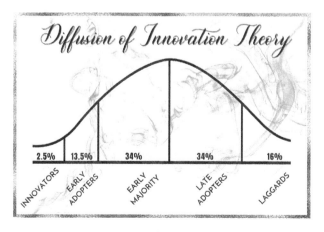

- We don't know people who would donate real estate. In other words, we don't understand this. It is ridiculous to believe people would just hand over a deed, and because it wasn't our idea, we will pass.

Champions can take a stand at any stage of an innovative shift in consciousness. According to the bell curve, you will see we are currently in the "Early Adopters" phase. Isn't it interesting that charitable gifting of real estate makes up 2% of the funding that non-profits receive annually? And as you see here, those were the innovators of this idea. However, it's been "stuck" at that level for 100+ years because no one thought to bring it to the public.

UNTIL NOW. Until The REAL Agents of Change formed alliances all over the U.S. and Canada. Until the "What's Next?" was answered with the "5 Keys," the 7P's, this revolution, and this book. YOU can be THE CHAMPION in the early adopter's phase!

Keys 2, 3, 4, and 5 are for The Champions because it is here you are fighting for, speaking for, and battling for someone else or a cause you believe in. THAT is when you are "being" The Champion: "Doing" what The Champions would do. "Having" what The Champions have, which in our world is Legacy Listings that fund non-profits by the BILLIONS and "Making Money Making a Difference!"

The REAL Agents of Change

Video/Audio #17 of the following Section at:
www.theraoc.com/book#recording17

First 3 P's

15

Purpose
YOUR WHY

First 3 P's: Setting Intention and How You are Being Seen, Received, & Perceived

P #1: Purpose: YOUR Purpose

Why do you care about charitable gifting of real estate? Why do you want to talk about it? Why do you want others to know about it? Why do you want donors to donate and non-profits to get funded, enlarging their endowments sixfold?

If you are attracted to OUR tribe of "REAL Agents of Change," you are a good person. You are altruistic. You want to be a contribution. You want to be part of the solution and do the right thing.

WIIFY: What's In It For You?

- Do you want that one non-profit you've loved your whole life never to struggle for money again?
- Do you want ALL non-profits in your marketplace to see YOU as the specialist who helps them get funded?
- Would you love to double your assets under management (AUM) as a financial advisor?
- Would you like to be "The" resource provider, connector, and go-to "Networker" (NetWebber),

and build your business because of it?

- Would you like to attract 87% of your marketplace that would hire the attorney, Realtor, dog walker, or network marketer who is socially responsible?
- Would you like to be the company, product, or service provider who is socially responsible?
- Have you been a successful advisor for twenty years and are ready to be seen and heard in a new light?
- Do you want to have a Unique Sales Proposition that differentiates you from everyone else?
- Who do you want to talk to about CGRE? Who do you REALLY want to do business with, receive these donations from, or add to your center of Influence?
  - People looking for tax breaks
  - Heart-centered folks who love animals
  - Families
  - Investors
  - Estate Attorneys
  - Financial Advisors
  - Realtors
  - Elderly
  - Business Owners
  - ...the list is endless

Do you admit that you want to "Make Money?" And if it's through/from/because of "Making a Difference," well, that's even better! The point is, when people ask me, "How do I talk to XYZ about this?" I say, "That depends. What's in it for you, and what's in it for them?" There needs to be more context. We have "canned" emails, social media posts, and scripts. We will share examples of these later in the book. However, to have a REAL Influence, Impact people, and Inspire interest and action on their part, doesn't it make sense to talk with them instead of at them?

THEIR WHY

P #2: Purpose: THEIR Purpose

Let's talk about what their purpose is. For example, say you are a fund-raiser for veterans. If you're talking to a donor who is a veteran and is always willing to roll his sleeves up in the trenches for his veteran brothers and sisters, it would be a very different conversation than with the board member who wants to earn brownie points and acknowledgment.

We talk about telling a story...tapping into the 4 S's as Dr. James shares...**Story, Story, Story, Stop talking**. So consider the different story versions in the following simple examples.

"John, I just found out we can serve thousands more veterans a year with the funding we need. Let's learn more about this together so our brothers and sisters get the care they need."

"Bill, non-profits like ours bring in millions of dollars without traditional fund-raisers. So, the opportunity for media coverage and for you to be interviewed on the local news is huge."

The above are modest examples of extremely different purposes and perspectives or **WIIFT** (**W**hat's **I**n **I**t **F**or **T**hem) for you to consider as you think of the clients you have, your friends and family, the people on your board, and those in your networking groups. Can you see how different people and personalities require a different story, not a canned script?

Presence

YOUR INNER GAME

P #3: Presence

How do you feel inside? Your INNER game. Who are you being in the conversation? When people attend our charitable real estate masterclass, they see, hear, learn, and understand that CGRE is a life changer! They know it has been around for 100+ years and $9 billion a year funds non-profits. The case studies we share gives examples of many types of property, situations for donors, and amounts of donations that it is simply an exciting topic of conversation to have with their "Top 10." Their "presence," posture, confidence, and commitment to the conversations are high. This enthusiasm comes through their voice, body language, and knowing that this IS "The Awakening" the non-profit world is experiencing right now.

To have the most Influence and Impact on those you are communicating with, the only one who needs to be "sold" is you! After all:

- If you are not sold, they won't be sold.
- If you are not buying it, they will never buy it.

One of the many benefits of finding this unicorn way to merge real estate with REAL change is that we can finally take off our salesperson hat—**No more "convincing" people.** We truly are agents of change, bearing information and education so those we communicate with can see the opportunities for themselves.

As the Influencer, Advisor, or Fund-raiser, the best news you can receive from this book is: **There is no selling, convincing, or talking people into donating real estate.** You don't need to convince people to accept a large check from the donation of real estate. You simply have the ability to shift their mindset and actions from "FundRAISING" to "FUNRaising" or getting "FUNded."

People are open, or they are not. They are looking to "Give Smarter," or they are not. They either want a tax deduction, or they don't. They either want to help their donors give generously, or they do not. Our job is to educate everyone about this opportunity. Sure, there are PLENTY of questions to answer for clarification. Everyone deserves to know that charitable gifting of real estate is an option whether they are a property owner, a non-profit, an advisor, or any of those who serve them. And that is the point we are making.

They deserve to know and understand, not be sold on it or convinced it is a good idea for them. This is why your presence in the conversation is important and why we are taking this much time on "P3." Show up in your communication as a confident message carrier coming from your heart, not a convincing salesperson all up in your head, and you'll see the difference in the response.

The next 4 P's are more advanced and come into play in Key #4: Leverage. Do not be overwhelmed. You can Lead Generate without the last 4 P's. However, we intend to share the process from start to finish, so the full concept is clear.

The REAL Agents of Change

Video/Audio #18 of the following Section at:
www.theraoc.com/book#recording18

Second 3 P's Positioning and Partnering

16

Positioning

HOW YOU SHOW UP

Second 3 P's: Paying Attention and What You are Doing
P #4: Positioning

How do you show up? How are you perceived and received? What are peoples' first impressions of you? How do people see you, your organization, and your company? If a quick search was done online, how would you be received and perceived by the searcher?

We will assume that because you have made it this far in the book, you have a desire to position yourself with charitable real estate in some fashion. As a non-profit, you'll want to start letting your friends, followers, fans, and funders know they can benefit from gifts of real estate. You can do this by announcing it on your website, newsletters, emails, and social media posts.

Do not make the mistake of having it as an "oh by the way" at the bottom of your newsletter! Instead, create a whole newsletter about it. Be loud and proud that your non-profit is a visionary committed to your mission by taking BOLD action!

As Influencers and Advisors, that is good advice for you too! So insert your title once you have taken the class and the test that certifies you as a "Certified Charitable Real Estate Specialist

(C.C.R.E.S)." You are an exclusive group of socially responsible advisors who help your clients give smarter, your causes receive six times their endowments, and your community becomes a better place because you took action on the "Secret **Real Estate Niche that is Funding Non-profits by the Billions!"**

Does your title position you with that Unique Sales Proposition (USP) when you show up? When people ask you, "What do you do?" have some fun with your answer!

- "I strategize with high-net-worth philanthropic people who give smarter and avoid capital gains taxes. Who do you know like that?"
- "As the first Charitable Real Estate Specialist in NYC, I love collaborating with non-profits to get them funded in the millions. Who do you know that are decision-makers of non-profits?"
- "Our non-profit partners with Realtors to list real estate donations that we can receive from any-where in the country. What Realtors do you know who want more listings?"
- "I help visionary non-profits find hundreds of millions of dollars in funding from the supporters they already have. Whose board would you like me to speak with to make that happen for them?"
- "We collaborate with seasoned real estate professionals, giving FULL Commission listings that benefit their communities by the millions of dollars. Do you know any influential Realtors who would like to mingle with hundreds of non-profits in their marketplace?"

For some examples of what you could be leveraging to position yourself on social media, zoom, business cards, etc., visit www.theraoc.com/book#samples.

WHO & WHY

P #5: Partnering: Who and Why

Now comes the FUN part of the getting FUNded and FUNdraising! It is much more fun, efficient, and effective to have others playing, partnering, and promoting with you. There are lots of partner categories. Think of your partners as those who would benefit *you* and **who can benefit themselves from CGRE.** Also, who would benefit from the promotion and social interactions because of leveraging CGRE in their marketing, and because of you?

The first partners are always real estate focused businesses. After all, we are talking about funding non-profits through real estate. We will give a handful of examples below, then invite you to go to a full list of hundreds of examples in our "Partner Profiles" list. This is also a great time to invite you to pick up a pen and some paper to begin creating a list of people who come to your mind. After all:

Knowledge is not power until it is applied.
Applied knowledge is empowering.

Partners: Real Estate Related Businesses
- Mortgage
- Title
- Insurance
- Home Inspectors
- Stagers
- Appraisers

Download the Partner Profile list document.
www.theraoc.com/book

Let's go through an example and think of how this relates to your cause, career, company, and potential clients. We could do this example with partners who would benefit from and resonate with children's issues, animals, health, education, the elderly, the environment...the list goes on and on. However, for the following example, we will use veteran causes.

Partners: Realtors Who Are Veterans or Support Veterans
These partners can be an ARMY of Realtors Locally or Nationwide for a non-profit!

Partners: Veteran Non-profits in Your Market
- The Journey Home
- Mission 22
- Hope for the Warriors

116

Partners: Veteran-Owned Businesses
- Plumbers
- Contractors
- Warehouses
- Manufacturers
- Coffee shop owners
- Print shop owners

Partners: Businesses Who Support Veterans
Give them free coffee or discounts or do fundraising events like poker runs.

Partners: Veteran Doctors
- VA Hospital
- Specialist with PTSD
- Therapist

Partners: Businesses Who Cater to Veterans because You Suggest It
- Extreme sports
- Camping
- Adventure
- Motorcycle shops

Partners: Veterans Themselves
These could be property donors or anyone who can share on social media or hand out a flyer.

Partners: Your Past and Current Clients
If you are an advisor, they're your clients. If you are a non-profit, they are your donors and those you serve.

Partners: Your center of influence
- Friends
- Family
- Fans
- Followers
- Funders
- Business network

Partners: Affiliates and Vendors
Think of who you pay for services to run your organization.
- Office cleaning staff
- Landscaper
- Office furniture

Partners:
- Contractors
- Staff
- Team members
- Employees
- Receptionist
- Admin
- Office manager
- Other advisors
- Salespeople

Partners: Volunteers
Whoever takes the time to serve you for free is passionate about your cause. In the "Cause Marketing Campaigns" section in Key 4: Leverage, we will discuss what to do with these partners. As you can see, there are many people to partner with. However, why they would partner with you depends on **their Purpose or WIIFT.**

The REAL Agents of Change

Video/Audio #19 of the following Section at:
www.theraoc.com/book#recording19

Second 3 P's Continues with P6 Promoting

17

We invite you to think this through. Why would mortgage companies, title companies, Realtors, whole real estate companies, plumbers, print shops, or Main St USA businesses benefit from being socially responsible and helping hundreds of non-profits they love get funded by the millions? To see what's in it for them as an overall business development element will be key to doing a full-blown Cause Marketing Campaign. It is super helpful to know individually, what is in it for each person emotionally, spiritually, and financially. However, getting the overall concept that attracting 87% of their market from being seen as socially responsible is key to your campaigns.

TOGETHER & INDIVIDUALLY

P #6: Promoting: Individually and Together
Promoting can take many forms. It can be a simple one-on-one conversation, an email blast, social media posts, being interviewed on podcasts or the media, Facebook lives, you being the interviewer, or any form of being seen and heard.

As we like to say at The RAOC, **"Whether you want to be "Superman" in front of the cameras or "Clark Kent" behind the scenes, there is a place for your time, talent, and treasure when promoting CGRE."**

Like Clark Kent's alter ego is Superman, and Batman has Robin, here at The RAOC, we have Lady Legacy (Cami) and Donation Diva (Danielle)!

Lady Legacy is seen and heard in front of the camera. She is the face and voice of the revolution and blazing the trail for all to join! Yet without Donation Diva supporting Lady Legacy by creating platforms, marketing pieces, logos, designs, and all things system related, Lady Legacy could not hold up the "Key" that Revolutionizes the funding, tax deductions, and full

commission listings —ultimately revolutionizing a smarter, more fun, efficient, and effective way for all to obtain their payoffs!

It takes a tribe to create the "Positioning, Partnering, and Promoting" involved in transforming how people do something this important and impactful! We need ALL the talented people and what they bring to the table. So we welcome you to support this revolution in your way!

When we start reverse engineering the 7 P's from Purpose to Payoff ™, you'll see how connected and collaborative promoting and partnering is. Whether you are the Influencer, Advisor, or Fund-raiser, your payoffs come from promoting what you are "DOING" in the world—not so much what you "do." In other words, everyone knows a Realtor, an estate planning attorney, a financial advisor, a mechanic, a network marketer, a fund-raiser, etc. So, what you do, lots of people do. However, what you are "doing" in the world is unique and comes from a place of passion, caring, and purpose, which will leave people touched and inspired to become involved in your campaign. (This, too, will be further discussed in Key 4: Leverage.)

Find examples of emails, social media, and videos we leverage to promote at www.theraoc.com/book#samples.

The REAL Agents of Change

Video/Audio #20 of the following Section at:
www.theraoc.com/book#recording20

The 7th P: The Payoff

18

THE 4 "I"S
INFLUENCE, IMPACT, INCOME & INSPIRATION

P #7: Payoff: The 4 I's: Influence, Impact, Income, & Inspiration

When putting this system together, this final P was suggested to be "Paycheck." However, there is way more to what we receive and want to produce, obtain, create, feel, and be, do, and have than just a paycheck.

Payoff Definitions

- The return on investment (ROI) or a bet
- A final outcome; a conclusion
- The climax of an incident or enterprise
- A decisive fact or factor resolving a situation or bringing about a definitive conclusion

These are what we mean by the payoff. So, what is the "ROI" you want at the conclusion of the 7 P's from Purpose to Payoff ™? What ROI do you want from your time, talent, and treasure? What ROI do you want for taking action to implement Charitable Gifting of Real Estate into your business plan? Whether you are the Influencer, advisor, fund-raiser, property donor, Realtor, financial professional, CPA, attorney, visionary leader, or non-profit from the largest to the smallest, what do you want to achieve here?

We break the Payoff down into the 4 I's.

- Influence
- Impact
- Income
- Inspiration

We are all looking for these four I's at some level—especially those of you who are still with us in this book. So, the invitation here is to consider and write out your 4 I's in detail. I'll share my personal 4 I's here with you as an example.

Influence

- Influencing a non-profit to take action
- Influencing a group of young girls to become philanthropic
- Influencing a real estate investor group to implement charitable gifting of real estate in their community to help bring awareness to the revolution.

Who we want to influence can be one, many, or all! For Cami C.E. Baker, it is to influence a full shift of thinking on how non-profits are funded. When I saw how untapped this niche is and thought of the thousands of people in real estate, I knew I wanted to influence at least 1% of them to be BOLD and take action! I wanted to be the Influencer who brings awareness and awakens The Giant within, as Tony Robbins would say!

The Influence I am is on the 5% of Influencers, advisors, and fund-raisers that resonate with my style and message so they, in turn, can be an Influencer for their causes, communities, and companies. It is the trickle-down effect. I know that I am not for everyone! However, I am also clear that those I reach will reach those I do not.

I take this responsibility very seriously. I am grateful that the filter I was listening through in that initial conference was such that I saw the puzzle pieces come together to create a beautiful vision of funding for all non-profits, one real estate professional (or real estate company) at a time. Now my vision has expanded to include Influencers, advisors, and visionary fund-raisers seeking to Leave a Legacy.

So, what influence do you want to have? Imagine it. Write it. TAKE ACTION!

Impact

Your impact could be on your neighborhood, town, state, region, country, or world. It could be one person, a group of people, one non-profit, all kids, or the elderly. In other words, YOU get to decide what impact you want to have and on who.

My impact is having Certified Charitable Real Estate Specialist (C.C.R.E.S.) and Charitable Real Estate Divisions (C.R.E.D.) in every city/area/marketplace of our country by 2025.

From Resistance to Acceptance to The Norm

In the early 2000s, when I was a real estate agent, I had a client say to me, "Cami, my daughter owns a house that she owes more than it is worth. I need you to help her." To which I responded, "What the hell do you want me to do if she owes more than it's worth?" She replied, "There was something in the '80s called a 'workout' or 'short sale,' look into it."

When I googled "short sale," the only information I found was how Victoria's Secret was having a sale on shorts! No joke!

If I had known at that moment, what I learned six months later, I would have acquired ShortSales.com, NHShortSales.com, HowToDoShortSales.com, FLShortSales.com... You get the point. No one, including the banks doing them, knew what a short sale was at that time. Now, the average person has an idea of what it is and knows someone who has been in a short sale situation.

The Legacy Impact I will leave is that charitable gifts of real estate are simply the norm by the time my life is over. That it is REVOLUTIONIZED! That it is not a foreign concept, and when you say, "charitable gifts of real estate," the average person will say, "Oh yeah, our church just built a new parish from one of those." or "My sister is a Realtor. That's her specialty."

Income

Believe it or not, I am not money motivated. Being "Mission Motivated" can make it challenging to dream up income goals. I tend to look *at who I want to help more than how much money I want to make.* However, I once had a mentor who said, "When you know how many people a month you want to help, and you know the average revenue generated from helping each person, you can create your business plan based on the number of people served."

When I consider all the business development elements The RAOC has in place, and all those who will be served, the income streams are endless. The following are ways The RAOC and I are "Making Money" because of "Making a Difference." So, consider how some of them can develop your business and generate income.

Information

- Public Facebook Group
  www.facebook.com/groups/therealagentsofchange
- 25-Minute "The RAOC Revolution, Charitable Real
  Estate 101 Overview"
- Library of videos of quick FAQ
- The REAL Agents of Change Interview Series
- Media coverage
- The RAOC being interviewed
- The RAOC interviewing others

Education

- Charitable Real Estate Masterclass
- The Legacy Launch-pad
- Custom Cause Marketing Campaigns
- Workshops
- Retreats
- Private Facebook Group

Certification

- Certified Charitable Real Estate Specialist
  (C.C.R.E.S.)
- Charitable Real Estate Division C.R.E.D. and its
  C.R.E.D.ibility

Resources, Relationships, and Revenue that RAOC

- The Legacy Listings provide referral
  and marketing fees
- Speaking engagements
- Sponsorship
- Affiliate partnerships
- Book sales
- Real Estate is HOT, Fundraising is NOT online sales

- Speaking engagements book sales
- Real Estate Companies and Financial Institutions provide a copy to all their advisors
- Books for "Fund-raisers" or "Awareness Raisers" that lead to funding

All the above tallies up to $100,000 a month within two years of writing this book.

If you're interested in joining our revolution as an affiliate, you can get 10% as a C.R.E. Specialist or 25% as a C.R.E. Champion back from any course purchased by your contacts. For more info, visit www.TheRAOC.com/Book.

Even more important than our income is all the Billions of dollars for the non-profits and millions for the advisory community, which benefits ALL communities worldwide.

What a WIN-WIN-WIN we have our hands-on! The goal of The REAL Agents of Change is to add $1 Billion a year in donations to non-profits through gifts of real estate.

If conservatively the $1 Billion a year is all equity and the actual amount of The Legacy Listings, that is roughly $50 Million in commission to real estate professionals; or more if The Legacy Listings are listed much higher to result in the $1 Billion in equity. Not to mention all the fees our professional financial friends will earn, as this "hard asset," the one asset they cannot manage, is liquidated.

The donor can pull cash from the property to buy stock, life insurance, and other products they sell. The total donation can be put in a "Donor Advised Fund (DAF)" that requires management. Not all financial advisors are "Certified Charitable Real Estate Specialists," so The RAOC team will attract more high-net-worth clients and retain their clients' children as clients when assets are in a DAF they can manage into the next generation. Also, keep in mind that 87% of the population is already choosing the company, product, or service provider who is socially responsible—giving all partners the advantage to "Position, Partner, and Promote" with The RAOC!

As you can see, adding income as an Influencer, advisor, or fund-raiser is not a problem. You will just want to think this part through and know you can add a zero or two to your bot- tom line with the right strategies.

What income do you want to have? Really think it through. Reading this book gives you great ideas about how CGRE adds income, but writing down your ideas and declaring your actions to achieve new income thresholds is empowering!

The REAL Agents of Change

Video/Audio #21 of The Following Section at:
www.theraoc.com/book#recording21

Ooohh...The Inspiration

19

Inspiration

Oooohhh boy...What a great feeling to **BE Inspired! To BE an Inspiration! To Inspire others to Be, Do, and Have anything they want!**

The REAL Agents of Change we attract tend to be exactly that...REAL Agents of Change who love helping people and want to do big things in the world. They are inspired people who live to inspire others! So, when someone is full of inspiration, and you sprinkle them with the ability to fund non-profits by the BILLIONS, help their fellow businesspeople make money through making a difference, and educate them to "Give Smarter" to those they care about (instead of the government), mountains are moved, paradigms are shifted, and differences are made.

I am absolutely humbled when someone tells me that I inspire them. I know being an inspiration to others is a huge responsibility. I have an ex-husband who taught me the phrase: **To whom much is given, much is expected.**

My Payoff is how I inspire others to TAKE ACTION through The REAL Agents of Change and all the good we are doing in the world. Traveling the country in my RV inspires others to step into doing what excites them. The adoption of my rescue animal saves the lives of thousands more by inspiring others to do the same. Even more, I want to inspire others not to have a "bucket list." Stop the one day, maybe someday, they will do it. Instead, DO IT NOW!

It turns me on—lights my fire—knowing that what we are doing every day inspires non-profits to be bold in unchartered waters. Also, it inspires seasoned real estate professionals who are bored with the same-ole, same-ole to **Step Up, Step Out, and Step Into** a new way of being seen in their marketplace. I've had beautiful, well-established real estate agents tell me that after years in business, becoming a Certified Charitable Real Estate Specialist (C.C.R.E.S.) has reignited a passion in them that they didn't think was possible! **I am living the *Payoffs* every day, and that is what I am Inspired to Inspire in YOU!**

Reverse Engineering the 7 P's from Purpose to Payoff™

Now that you know the 7 P's, here is the deal. To Be, Do, and Have the **Payoffs** you want, doesn't it make sense that it would serve you to **Promote** what you're doing? Not what you "do," but what you are "Doing" in the world? And instead of **Promoting** all by yourself, wouldn't it be more fun, efficient, and effective to **Promote** with **Partners**? However, you cannot look for **Partners** until you are **Positioned**; because we already know people will google, stalk, creep, or research you. So, you better have outstanding **Positioning**. You won't

Position yourself properly if your **Presence** is wishy-washy. No one else will be either if you are not "sold out" or "buying into" what you are doing. Furthermore, you cannot get your **Presence** solid if you are not certain of WIIFT...what their **Purpose** is. Lastly, you won't know who to talk to, what to say, or how to say it from their perspective if you don't know your **Purpose.**

SSHHWWEEE...**Got it?!**

The REAL Agents of Change

Video/Audio #22 of the following Section at:
www.theraoc.com/book#recording22

First Action Step

20

What's YOUR Purpose? What's THEIR Purpose?
What's Your Presence?

Let the Lead Generating begin! The focus in Key #2: Lead Generation is on the first 3 P's. Here is where it's time for you to pick up a pen and paper. Of course, you can do it by typing if you must, but something magical happens when you engage your brain through writing.

You are more focused when you write versus typing.

The First Real Action Steps to Leverage Real Estate for REAL Change.

- What is YOUR Purpose?
- WHY are you interested in charitable gifting of real estate?
- What do you want to do with it?

In your why or purpose, be thinking of who you want to talk to about charitable gifting of real estate? There can be many categories of people. Let's pick an example for this exercise.

Let's say you are a fund-raiser, and you know you want to share the story with your donors. Also, let's say you see the benefit in sharing this with Realtors and financial professionals. That would be three categories of people, right? We challenge you to consider that this represents at LEAST six groups of people:

1. Donors who are altruistic and love your cause
2. Donors who are numbers-oriented and resonate with tax benefits
3. Realtors who are heart-centered and love doing the right thing

143

4. Realtors who are looking for business and would want to know about getting a FULL Commission to list and liquidate The Legacy Listings
5. Financial professionals who are community-focused and want to help their clients be more philanthropic
6. Financial professionals who want to learn how to add Assets Under Management to their book of business

All these people will benefit from hearing the story and learning about charitable gifting of real estate. However, are you starting to see that you want to consider P2: THEIR Purpose (or WIIFT) as you have these conversations?

This isn't to say you can't send one big email campaign blast to everyone. And, of course, social media posts are seen by thousands of people and can be very general or completely focused on a target audience. Also, this is not saying you need six different campaigns to reach all six categories of people.

We are suggesting that right this red-hot minute, as you are learning about this yourself, you take time to honor those you want to communicate with, knowing that how you approach people depends on what you know about them, their communication style, and WIIFT. This also suggests that the first people you want to share this with are those you know best. Those who you already know what makes them tick, what turns them on, and at the very least, if they are heart-centered or money-motivated.

Yes, lead generation can include emails and social media, BUT who are your Top 10? This could be your Top 3, Top 10, Top 20, or Top 50 in any of the six categories. It depends on how much Influence, Impact, Income, and Inspiration you want to stir up. You may only know four Realtors and three financial professionals but have 300 donors to talk to. The list of the six categories is just a memory jogger and a means to get you started.

To be GREAT at anything, you first need to be good. To be good at it, you first need to be bad at it. To be bad at it, you first need to get started! So, let's get started in order to be GREAT!

The REAL Agents of Change

Video/Audio #23 of the following Section at:
www.theraoc.com/book#recording23

WARM Market vs. COLD Market

21

WARM Market vs. COLD Market

This topic is extremely important! As Dr. James mentioned in the Foreword of this book, sometimes you will get a little kick in the rear.

- Do not fall into the lack mentality that you don't
- Know anyone who will donate real estate.
- Do not make decisions for other people by choosing who to share this blessing and information with.
- Do not treat this any differently than a good movie,
  a great new restaurant, or other "fundraising" tool. You have, would, and always do, tell people about those things.
- Do not rob non-profits of millions (BILLIONS) in funding.
- Do not let animals, children, universities, churches, and all those who will be fed, housed, educated, and saved, suffer because you didn't share this with the people you know.
- Do not hold back on giving your clients and donors the opportunity to have tax deductions. Give smarter and LEAVE A LEGACY NOW.
- Do not hoard information that can double the profitability of the real estate industry, financial professionals, and businesses that make a living supporting and serving your community.
- Do not assume you know what is best for others.

We all know what happens when we "ass-u-me" anything.

This entire book is about **Warm Market Communication**. You can buy email lists of thousands of Realtors. You can cold call financial professionals off LinkedIn. You can pay a company to find donors who own lots of property and tend to give to your type of cause. Yes, you can do those things, and maybe six months from now (or next year), it would be a good use of budget and marketing dollars. However,

- Have integrity
- Take a stand for those you say you are here to serve
- Your friends, family, followers, funders, and the foundation of your community
  - Deserve to know
  - Need to know their options
  - Will be grateful you thought enough of them to inform and educate them
  - Will introduce you to high-net-worth, generous, multiple property owners, non-profits, Realtors, and all those THEY know who deserve to know, need to know, and will be grateful THEY introduced YOU!

One more thing to consider here...

- YOUR Donors are on OTHER donors' lists.
- YOUR clients know other people in your industry.
- YOUR friends, family, followers, and funders will be hearing about this, whether it is from you, the other non-profits they support, or the other Realtors in your marketplace. In other words, YOU can be the one who takes The Legacy Listing and funds your community by the millions, or it will simply be someone else.

This time next year, you will either be saying:

- "Wow, look at all the funds flowing from me taking action!"

OR

- "Oops, I'm glad my community is getting funded and served, but boy does it stink that the other non-profit Realtor is getting real estate donations from people on my list!"

People ask all the time, "What's Next?" Sometimes what they mean is, "How much does this cost?" Friends, what we share here is freely given to move the revolution forward. The cost is huge if you do not pay it forward yourself. Why wouldn't you first want to tell those you love and who love you most?

Of course, we get compensated for sharing our brilliance, value, marketing material, resources, strategies, and business-building techniques. No one else in the world is better at this than The REAL Agents of Change. We have systems, scripts, support, and the only mindset, marketing, and mentors who specialize in how to Leverage Real Estate for REAL Change.

It all starts with communicating with other human beings. So, let's start with the ones you say you'd like to serve and support...THAT is FREE.

The REAL Agents of Change

Video/Audio #24 of the following Section at:
www.theraoc.com/book#recording24

Your Top 10 Lists

22

Top 10 Memory Jogger List

Here is another memory jogger to get you started. In addition, there are extensive Top 10 Lists to review based on the categories here.

www.theraoc.com/book.

You may know two in one category, three in another, or 1,000 in another. Remember, as you read, listen to, or watch the information from this book, hundreds of thousands of people are consuming this information, too. As we discussed above, your Top 10 altruistic donors are ALSO on other non-profit lists, just like every category mentioned below. Others in your industry and marketplace are doing this same exercise! So, time is of the essence! The clock is ticking! The REAL Agents of Change will be meeting and mingling with your contacts, whether we meet them through you or not. This IS happening, with or without you, and with or without us. So, let's "Position, Partner, and Promote" together to make sure all our payoffs are realized.

Our Mission is to Fund Your Mission

Our Purpose is to Fund Your Purpose

Our Business is Funding Your Business

How It Happens

- Top 10 Altruistic Donors
- Top 10 Numbers-Focused Donors
- Top 10 Volunteers
- Top 10 Past Clients
- Top 10 Realtors
- Top 10 Financial Advisors
- Top 10 Property Managers
- Top 10 Non-profits
- Top 10 Influencers
- Top 10 Property Owners
- Top 10 Center of Influence
- Top 10 Real Estate Related Businesses
- Top 10 Animal Lovers
- Top 10 Children Advocates
- Top 10 Environmentalist
- Top 10 Senior Care Businesses
- Top 10 Health Care Providers
- Top 10 Veterans
- Top 10 Religious affiliations
- Top 10 University affiliations
- Top 10 People who love to recycle
- Top 10 People who want to change the world
- Top 10 People who are talking about starting a non-profit
- Top 10 People who are healthy and talk about health
- Top 10 People who are retired
- Top 10 Seniors

The REAL Agents of Change

Video/Audio #25 of the following Section at:
www.theraoc.com/book#recording25

WHO, WHAT, and HOW...Let's Plant Seeds

23

WHO to Talk To, WHAT to Say, and HOW to Say It

Now that you know YOUR purpose, you understand it helps to know THEIR Purpose and you have a list of WHO to talk to. So, let's talk about WHAT to say and HOW to say it.

The what to say and how to say it leads us back to P3: Your Presence. When I was training Realtors on how to call expired listings and For Sale By Owners (FSBOs), they always asked, "What do I say when they ask me what my commission is?" and "What do I say when they say they know another Realtor?" Or any number of other questions they would want "canned." Here are the magic responses.

My question to the Realtor would be, "That depends on where you are in the conversation, if you have a rapport with them, and most importantly, what is their motivation? WHY are they selling? Because all the fancy lingo, scripts, and words won't matter if the person is not motivated. On the flip side, **if they ARE motivated, you don't need fancy language. You just need to ask the right questions and be PRESENT in the conversation to hear them and respond accordingly.**

The best way to lead-generate, start the ball rolling, and get your cause, community, and company buzzing about this HOT TOPIC is to make a list of people and share the story. However, we know it is too vague, so in the next section there is a quick and easy solution...action steps to take, if you will.

The REAL Agents of Change

Video/Audio #26 of the following Section at:
www.theraoc.com/book#recording26

Simple Script

24

This system came to us when we were working with a very large non-profit that had been sending out a three-piece campaign about charitable gifts of real estate but was not getting much response. They had three hundred thousand donors and paid a company to whittle the list down to those who owned multiple pieces of property, were in the right age range, and were most likely to be a candidate for donating real estate. The marketing pieces went to 8,000 people, and only one person had ever "responded." We suggested they follow up with a phone call to invite the potential donor to a live online presentation to learn more.

They had 25 employees who held the title of *"fund-raiser."* There were already reaching out to all the donors with the typical fundraising conversation. So, these fund-raisers knew the couple hundred from this list they each were calling.

The campaign consisted of a physical mailer, a follow-up post-card, and a follow-up email. (Don't worry, we won't suggest this much out-of-pocket expense.) We suggested that the fourth part of the campaign be a conversation like this:

"Hi, Bill. This is Teresa at XYZ non-profit. (Insert pleasantries.) I'm calling to see if you received our recent mailing. (yes/no) It has a fascinating story about how non-profits, just like ours, are getting funded, frankly by the millions, all over the country. Supporters like you are invited to learn how to "Give Smarter" and have hefty tax advantages from major gifts of assets. I don't know all the details, Bill, but we are hosting a 30- 45 minute live gathering online, and I thought of you. I knew you'd want to be in the know. Shall I email or text you the link?"

163

Now in that example, Bill is a numbers guy. It could also go like this:

"Hi Larry, this is Teresa at XYZ non-profit. (Insert pleasantries.) I'm calling to see if you received our recent mailing. (yes/no) It has a fascinating story about how non-profits like ours receive the funds they need to serve their community. We are talking about millions of dollars that would help us save thousands more animals a year! Supporters like you are being invited to learn how to "Give Smarter" and truly have the impact they want from major gifts of assets. I don't know all the details, Larry, but we are hosting a 30-45 minute live gathering online, and because of your passion for our mission, I knew you'd want to be invited. Shall I email or text you the link?"

Notice how we shared the same story, just with the perspective the individual would relate to. **We are talking with them, not at them, with the WIIFT in mind.**

#1 This gives the person making the call a "reason" for calling as they are following up on previously sent messages to make sure the person received the postcard or email.

FYI: It doesn't matter if they have seen the email or post. It's just a fun and easy way to segway into the conversation.

#2 This gives the person making the call a "call to action" because they are inviting them to come to learn more.

Some of you do not need a "reason" or a "call to action" to pick up the phone and chat people up. However, this simple system is something anyone can follow and a plan of action with an end result. The "End Result" ultimately has "The Legacy Listing" donated. But those do not happen without first planting seeds, sharing information, and giving others the blessing of knowledge, options, and insight. The "End Result" starts with a simple "Yes" to wanting more information. So, in your initial communication, you want a "Yes!" to learn more.

KISS...Keep It Simple, Sweetie

We are not asking for real estate donations or if a non-profit wants to put us in front of their 10,000 donors. We are inviting people to become knowledgeable. That is all!

The REAL Agents of Change

Video/Audio #27 of the following Section at:
www.theraoc.com/book#recording27

The Legacy Launch-pad (™) Process

25

The Process of The Legacy Launch-pad ™

Schedule
- The RAOC Revolution, Charitable Real Estate 101
- This is a live online presentation
- Presented by your C.C.R.E.S. expert
- Schedule it two weeks out

Send three emails over two weeks
- Giving a little taste of the topic
- Inviting them to learn more
- Provide a video
- Provide a link to register easily

Post 3 social media invitations over two weeks
- Give a little taste of the topic
- Invite them to learn more
- Provide a video
- Provide a link to register easily

PERSONALLY CONTACT at least twenty people—more if you take this seriously—to invite them using the basic script from the previous section. Remember, numbers are perfect; people are not. If you want ten people to attend, you need twenty yeses. To get twenty yeses, you'll need to TALK with forty people. So do your math as to how big of an impact you want to have.

Host the live online presentation with your C.C.R.E.S. expert and send the recording to those in attendance and those who couldn't make it. Share the supporting material found below.

- **Q&A Video Library:**
  www.theraoc.com/book#faqs

- **CRES Class Link:**
  www.theraoc.com/book#masterclass

- **CGRE Road-map:**
  www.theraoc.com/book#road-map

- **Property Evaluation Form:**
  www.theraoc.com/book#propertyevaluation

And, of course, follow up and follow through!

Example of the 30-45 minute live gathering you can invite people to: www.theraoc.com/book#101

Example emails and social media that can be leveraged to invite them to the presentation: www.theraoc.com/book

There are full training modules and training videos on all topics around this.

- Who to invite
- *What to say and how to say it* in the email, social media, and verbal invitation
- Scripts for phone calls
- How to handle questions you cannot answer
- What to do to follow up after the presentation
- How to keep the momentum going after the presentation
- How to "Position, Partner, and Promote" these presentations to have a "Cause Marketing Campaign" that leverages The Legacy Listings for REAL Change

We know some people are chomping at the bit and just want to TALK TO PEOPLE without the emails and social media; that is AWESOME! If this is you, have at it! See below if you want to call people and send them a link.

- **The Library of Resources:**
  www.theraoc.com/book#faqs

- **The Pre-Recorded Presentation:**
  www.theraoc.com/book#101

- **Join in the LIVE presentation of Charitable Real Estate Masterclass: The Deep Dive LIVE on the 3rd Tuesday of every month:**
  www.theraoc.com/book#masterclass

- **If they have a property to be evaluated, they can fill out the form at:**
  www.theraoc.com/book#propertyevaluation

This Legacy Launch-pad ™ was created for those who want a simple system with steps to make it happen. It provides a way to "Launch" the creation of your "Legacy" in the first thirty days. This is a new, exciting, fresh, innovative conversation for everyone! When they ask questions you cannot answer, please remember our motto

Also, remember:

Confused people do nothing. Whether that confused person is you or the person you are sharing the story with. So please keep it simple and refer them to The RAOC and others who can be of service. For more

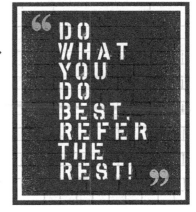

information on The Legacy Launch-pad™ and a description of all the marketing material it provides with lifetime access as we continue to add new content, go to: www.theraoc.com/store.

The REAL Agents of Change

Video/Audio #28 of the following Section at:
www.theraoc.com/book#recording28

Key #3 List and Liquidate, The Seed Analogy

26

Key #3: List and Liquidate
The Seed Analogy

Remember, we are not really "looking for leads" as much as we are "planting seeds." After all, who wants to be a "lead?" So, let's not look at people—human beings—as leads. We just use that word in the keys because that is what people are used to, and it fits the alliteration!

Some seeds are like sweet peas. You plant them, and they grow over a couple of months. So, in terms of planting and harvesting, you are eating very quickly.

Some seeds are like pumpkin seeds. They take months and months to bear fruit, but they feed you for a season.

Some seeds are like apple trees. These seeds take years and years to bear fruit, but they feed you for a lifetime and generations to come!

Some people you talk to about charitable gifting of real estate will have a piece of real estate they need evaluated right now, this very RED-HOT minute. It is simply perfect timing. They are ready, willing, and able to donate all or a portion of their property right away. They are sweet peas.

Some will need to hear it more than once. As you "plant the seed" and get them thinking, it may be the following year when they put it in their estate planning. They may know a non-profit that needs to hear about this right away, and that non-profit has donors they invite to learn more through "The Legacy Launch-pad." Through that process and over a short time, Legacy Listings come from the education. So, they have some sweet peas, but it feels like a pumpkin!

Some people, groups, organizations, causes, community foundations, and companies building culture may take a bit more nurturing...they are the apple trees! But, once they wrap their heads around the conversation, once they have their board meetings, get past the fundraising event they are currently doing, have their marketing team meet with The RAOC, and plan a campaign for next year, the apple blossoms are in bloom!

Just watch The Legacy Listings as they are Listed and Liquidated! Let's look at the numbers again. There is currently $9 Billion a year donated to non-profits through gifts of real estate. An average of $550,000 from one donation translates into 18,000 listings. And that number grows with every person who reads this book!

That's $24,657,534 and 44 Legacy Listings Listed a DAY!

$24,657,534 A DAY

Who do you know who needs, deserves, and would benefit from understanding how this works? Order your copies at 50% off to hand out to your cause, community, or company at info@theraoc.com.

The REAL Agents of Change

Video/Audio #29 of the following Section at:
www.theraoc.com/book#recording29

What is The Legacy Listing?

27

The Legacy Listing

These listings are just like any other real estate listing, from the perspective that the paperwork is the same for the Realtor. However, what makes them unique is that the proceeds go to the non-profit world!

Disclaimer: We are not CPAs, attorneys, or financial experts. We share how this works in layman's terms to keep it simple and easy for anyone to understand. We recommend you speak with independent counsel about your specific situation. While you're speaking with them, share this book because they too can be a Charitable Real Estate Specialist. We NEED them to help all our REAL Agents of Change and their clients with the numbers and specific scenarios!

The Legacy Listing Process

1. Property identified and evaluation form filled out
2. Property donor meets with the specialized non-profit
3. Net sheet examples are provided for the donor to make an educated business decision
4. The Donation Agreement is signed by the donor and specialized non-profit
5. "Charitable Gift/Donation" is made to specialized non-profit "Charitable Funds" are created by the specialized non-profit listing The Legacy Listing with a C.C.R.E.S. real estate agent to liquidate the gift and produce the proceeds or funds to be granted to the non-profit(s) designated in the donation agreement.

6. "Cause Marketing Campaign" implemented to "Position, Partner, and Promote" so that everyone involved receives the "Business Development Element" if they so choose.

For Profit AND Non-profit ARE Businesses and Benefit from These Campaigns

We acknowledge and respect the privacy of those who do not want to be mentioned in these campaigns. Anonymity is always a consideration. However, most of those who are part of this process love, want, desire, and are thrilled to receive the expo- sure created.

After all, "Real Estate is HOT, Fundraising is NOT, 5 Keys to Revolutionize How Charities & Champions Fund Their Causes, Careers, Companies & Communities" is all about how we, as a tribe, are bringing $1 Billion a year additional funding to the non-profit world via charitable gifts of real estate. This cannot happen without being seen and heard and educating the public about their options and opportunities to participate in "The Awakening" non-profits are experiencing by accepting non-cash assets.

When a **property is identified**, an evaluation form www.theraoc.com/book#propertyevaluation is filled out to ascertain the specifics and details of the property and the donor's intentions. Our specialized non-profits work with hundreds of non-profits, including Fidelity Charitables, the largest of the 1.3M 501c(3)'s in the US. These are reputable specialized non-profits that take their role in all of this very seriously. Nobody, including The ROAC, is interested in pulling one over on the government by taking advantage of the system. Our reputations are on the line, so the donor's intentions are the first questions asked. Under the right circumstances, the right donors have significant financial benefits when all the rules are followed. Assuming the property qualifies, the donor sees the advantage of making a charitable gift of real estate, and a donation agreement is created. Then we move forward.

The **donor donates** the property to the specialized non-profit. When the property is "Listed for sale," the "seller" is the specialized non-profit. We say The Legacy Listing agents receive a "FULL Commission" because they are all the sellers and want to incentivize the real estate community. We want to honor our real estate agent friends by paying them what they are worth, and we want this to be a WIN-WIN-WIN for EVERYONE involved. We want to make "doing good" a way of life!

The REAL Agents of Change

Video/Audio #30 of the following Section at:
www.theraoc.com/book#recording30

The Two-Step Process

28

A **donation of real estate is a two-step process:**

Step 1: Charitable Gifting
The donation is made to the specialized non-profit, a 501c(3).

- The property donor is immediately relieved of all responsibility for the property.
- Mortgages are paid off.
- CASH can be given to the property donor. (Bargain Sale described below.)
- Specialized Non-profit takes title along with financial responsibility.
- Property donor receives the benefit of the donation at that moment.
- This can be especially attractive towards the end of a calendar year when the donor needs the tax deduction, even though the property may not be listed or sold to the end-user until after the first of the next year.
  - Example: Donor makes the "Charitable Gift" December 15th, property listed December 16th, and is liquidated on February 15th the following year. The IRS recognizes the date of the donation for tax purposes as the Charitable Gift portion.

- IRS Form 8283 Non-cash Charitable Contributions:
  - Signed by three parties:
    - Appraiser (Amount and Date)
    - Donor
    - Non-profit (Specialized Non-profit)

Step 2: Charitable Funding.
- The real estate donation proceeds are procured and given to the non-profit world.
- The donation was Listed and Liquidated
- Proceeds are given to the non-profits the donor wants them to go to, whether that is a Donor Advised Fund (DAF), a non-profit directly, or multiple non-profits.
- Specialized non-profits (the ones we recommend) receives 2-10% of the proceeds, on average 5.9% in 2021.
- We can say "100% of the Proceeds go to non-profits" because the proceeds are split between non-profits the donor chooses and the specialized non-profit that handles the transaction.
- IRS Form 8282 Donor Information Return (if the property is sold within three years)
- Signed only by Specialized Non-profit

The first step is not a transaction that creates a commission. Essentially, the "title transfer" initiates the tax deduction. It is step two that requires a real estate agent. The "Charitable Gift" can be one of two scenarios.
- Outright Gift of the full value of the property
- Bargain Sale or Partial Gift, with some money exchanging hands
- Mortgage paid off
- Cash payment to the donor for any reason

Outright Gift

The property donor gives the property's full value to the non-profit and receives the "appraised value" as the basis of the write-off on their Adjusted Gross Income (AGI).

Example: The property appraises for $600,000. It sells for $550,000. The appraised value, not the sales price, is the basis of the tax deduction.

Bargain Sale or Partial Gift

Remember we said in the beginning that we want to keep this book simple and easy to understand? In all honesty, I had a difficult time with the term "Bargain Sale." First, it sounds like a "Bargain Basement Sale." Second, I didn't understand why this is the term used. Finally, it dawned on me about a year into hearing this term and using it myself to explain how this works. Fundamentally, the non-profit is "Buying" the property at a "bargain" price. Meaning if that same property valued at $600,000 had a $200,000 mortgage and the donor wants a $100,000 cash payment, then the non-profit is "buying" it for $300,000 and now has an asset it bought at a "bargain" and can liquidate to benefit from the remaining equity. Of course, they could keep the property they bought at a bargain, but the property is rarely donated to a non-profit that wants to manage, maintain, or move in. Suffice it to say, a bargain sale is anytime an amount of money is required to acquire a property.

This one caveat is a major reason so many of the 1.3M non-profits do not accept real estate or do it on a limited basis. Our simple scenario above would result in around $250,000 in cash to the non-profit world after expenses, but more was required to make it happen.

Are you starting to see why these specialized non-profits are so important?

If you are a non-profit that accepts real estate
- If it's local
- If it's mortgage-free
- If it's super simple and the donor has time to wait for board input and approval

AWESOME!

We applaud you for being a visionary and knowing that...

"CASH is NOT King when it comes to fundraising."
~ Dr. James

We encourage you to expand your "Ask." Knowing that when the seed you plant produces bigger, more complicated fruit in another state (or country), or something you would normally say "no" to, you now have your own "Charitable Real Estate Division (C.R.E.D.)" backing you!

The REAL Agents of Change

Video/Audio #31 of the following Section at:
www.theraoc.com/book#recording31

RAOC Testimony

29

Testimonial from REAL Agent of Change #2

We want to acknowledge Michael DiSchiavi, the REAL Agent of Change #2. The first after yours truly. He was the first real estate agent I called when I saw this and knew I would do something significant with it. Michael is featured as the example of the C.C.R.E.S. in the following section, CGRE Road-map. I've known Michael since 2009, and if ever there has been a heart-centered vision-driven human being, it is him.

In HIS words: "Put away the raffle tickets and bingo cards, cancel the costly gala. With CGRE, Cami Baker presents a way to largely fund non-profits and generously reward longtime donors—no more begging and pleading for a $20 check or a gift basket to be raffled off at some boring event that costs a lot of money. As a real estate professional, I can help worthy non-profits in my area simply by doing my job and getting paid what I am worth. Instead of the fair that raised $2,000 and took three months to put together, I can now bring in $550,000 with one transaction. It's a win-win-win. After all these years as a businessman and Realtor, I am finally having more unique conversations, getting listing leads, and having the opportunity to be a resource to many non-profits."

~ Michael DiSchiavi, Philanthropist, Entrepreneur, & Realtor
Michael DiSchiavi@exprealty.com
Facebook.com/Michael.Dischiavi.1
LinkedIn.com/in/michael-dischiavi-b4308b42
718-207-3792

The REAL Agents of Change

Video/Audio #32 of the following Section at:
www.theraoc.com/book#recording32

The CGRE Road-map Explained

30

The CGRE Road-map

Let's review the CGRE Road-map to see how simple this process is. You can find these on our website at:

www.theraoc.com/book#road-map

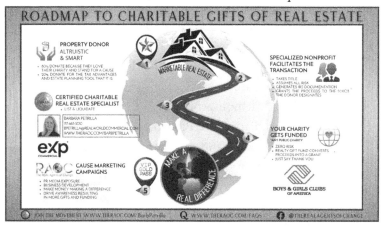

1. The donor wants to donate real estate. Why?
   a. Convenient (100% when done with 3rd party experts)
   b. Altruistic (80%)
   c. Tax Advantages (20%)
2. The donation goes to the Specialized Non-profit
   a. They take the title
   b. They pay off the mortgages
   c. They give cash when requested
   d. They produce the paper trail, and frankly, do the boring stuff that others don't want to do and don't understand. Basically, they make it easy, convenient, and doable for everyone involved.

3. Specialized Non-profit Lists the property with a C.C.R.E.S.
   a. C.C.R.E.S. understands this process
   b. C.C.R.E.S. has a way to "Position, Partner, and Promote" the donation
4. Specialized Non-profit cuts a check for the proceeds
   a. Listing has been liquidated
   b. Donor signed a "Donation Agreement" designating where the proceeds go
   c. Proceeds are dispersed in the form of "grants" to
   d. Donor-Advised Fund (DAF)
   e. A non-profit
   f. Multiple non-profits
5. Position, Partner, & Promote, Promote, Promote!
   a. PR, media, and exposure for this "Community Celebration"
   b. Educate the public that these donations are happening for these specific non-profits because of the C.C.R.E.S. or Advisors
   c. Share how the proceeds will benefit the community
   d. Let others know how THEY can benefit the non-profits THEY love
   e. Support THESE non-profits who are part of CGRE
   f. Work with THIS C.C.R.E.S.
   g. Work with THIS C.R.E.D. ... Charitable Real Estate Division...C.R.E.D.-ability...Do you have YOUR C.R.E.D.-ability!?

As you can see from all the marketing material provided, the certification created, and the revolution of The REAL Agents of Change empowering their marketplaces to bring this to their communities...knowing about CGRE and having a relationship with a specialized non-profit is great! It is a beginning. It is "Key #1: Learn." It gives the carrier of this knowledge the understanding and resources should the conversation of CGRE ever come up so they can be "Reactive" with the know-ledge and resources to handle a donation. However, your alliance with The REAL Agents of Change "The RAOC" pro- motes the "Proactive" ability to become a magnet for these donations! Becoming Proactive requires more than knowledge. After all, **Knowledge is not power until you are EMPOWERED with Action Steps to leverage that knowledge.**

The REAL Agents of Change

Video/Audio #33 of the following Section at:
www.theraoc.com/book#recording33

Key #4: Leverage

31

Key #4: Leverage
In the 7 P's from Purpose to Payoff™,
we discussed different kinds of Partners.

For example,
- Partners who are the typical real estate groupies
- Partners who are the non-profits in your chosen "niche"
- People, groups, organizations, and industries that can help you promote charitable gifting of real estate
- Those who are helped by being socially responsible
- Those with heart-centered exposure through a
- "Cause Marketing Campaign, CMC."

It brings so much joy to my heart to know these cause marketing campaigns we were doing for fund-raisers before the pandemic are now elevated to one thousand times their ability to:

"Make Money Making a Difference"
... through charitable gifting of real estate.

Until I learned about CGRE, I had spent years and years strategizing with financial services and real estate companies, entrepreneurs, Main St USA businesses, and small non-profits up to National and International 501c(3)'s (Ronald McDonald House and Make a Wish) addressing specific needs in the community with an "event" at the center of the campaign.

We did many car shows for numerous organizations all over the Northeast, "Bra Drives" for breast cancer awareness, and more events than I can list here to raise money or awareness of something important. Every event requires at least three months of planning, handing out fliers, asking for raffle items, selling raffle and gala tickets, and golf tournament four packs!

Bake Sales—BBQs—Ballroom Functions—Begging—Please help THIS cause over all the others! Please support THIS event! PLEASE put your corporate donation towards THIS sponsorship! And the next month, the next quarter, the next year, it's the same thing all over. So, it is the bucket vs. the pipeline analogy. We brought LOTS of buckets, did LOTS of good, and met LOTS of great people in the process. But let's face it, it was a $500 or $5,000 or $50,000 bucket that needed refilling constantly.

Maybe you can relate? Have you been on committees for months, door knocking for donations, or showing up to take tickets at the event? Or maybe you were the one donating the raffle item, buying the tickets, stroking the check for the auction item, or sponsoring the event. We have all done what we can on that level, and it may have warmed our hearts when the recipients came to the microphone to thank everyone for our efforts and share what this one-time check will do for their child, their family, their group home, their animal shelter or... their XYZ...you fill in the blank.

The REAL Agents of Change

Video/Audio #34 of the following Section at:
www.theraoc.com/book#recording34

What IF?

32

What if we were doing those events because we WANTED to, not because we HAD to. What if we were to gather with people because it is social and fun. We enjoy each other's company and celebrate life and what our organization is doing for the kids, veterans, the environment, and other wonderful causes? What if we built a pipeline of educated, informed donors who have all the information they need to make a good business decision for themselves and understand how to "Give Smarter." They can then leave their Legacy NOW and continue through the remaining chapters of their life, not just when they pass on.

There is a whole genre of people who need to know what to do with their accumulated real estate. They do not have children or heirs, or children who would be better served if their estate were not burdened by complicated real estate, and they need options as to what to do to uncomplicate their estates. Sure, they could just sell the property and give the non-profit the proceeds. But they would also be giving Uncle Sam a huge check, the majority of which would have gone to the non-profit or stayed in the property donors' pocket if they were to implement the charitable gifting of real estate.

There are hundreds of thousands of people RIGHT NOW who have a need THIS MONTH to donate real estate (sweet peas) and NEED to know their options. There are hundreds of thousands of people who, when in the pipeline because of our ability to educate them (pumpkins), would plan to simplify their estate over the next three years by making a charitable gift

209

of real estate. There are MILLIONS and MILLIONS... frankly, BILLIONS of dollars (apple trees) that will make their way into the non-profits' hands, hearts, and bank accounts that are part of "The Awakening" through major gifts of assets like real estate.

It is happening...It is already happening by $9 Billion a year. That number continues to grow and will double over time. The only question is, will you be a part of it?

Will YOUR cause get funded? Will YOUR community rally together to do "more good" with "more funding" because they embraced sharing posts and attending simple informational sessions? Imagine your community attending "FUN Raisers" and "Awareness Raisers" and TAKING ACTION because YOU inspired, invited, engaged, and enrolled them?

Will YOUR Career take off, and your friends, fans, family, and followers share what you are "doing" because you are socially responsible? When you are socially responsible, supporting causes your friends want you to support, it's not support coming out of your pocket. Instead, it's support that puts money in your pocket.

Will YOUR Company "Position, Partner, and Promote" you as socially responsible? And not just for one organization, but for multiple, dozens, or hundreds because charitable gifting of real estate shows us how even the non-profits can collaborate.

When the average donation is $550,000, and there are more than enough of these to go around, non-profits can share in the wealth and come together to support the "awareness raiser" to provide "FUNding," as opposed to the fund-raiser that provides one check.

By the way, it is OKAY to be profitable AND purposeful at

the same time! As a matter of fact, wouldn't you agree that whatever God or universal intelligence you believe in would want you to be abundant?

**Isn't it true that the more you have,
the more you can give?**

Let's be clear. You wouldn't be interested in The REAL Agents of Change or Legacy Listings or even a Revolution in how we all get funded unless you were a GOOD PERSON. So, we acknowledge you for the good person you are, AND celebrate and honor the good provider you are for your family, too! Do not ever feel guilt, shame, or uncomfortable wanting to "make money?"

The REAL Agents of Change

Video/Audio #35 of the following Section at:
www.theraoc.com/book#recording35

Position, Partner, & Promote

33

"Position, Partner, & Promote"

Do you and your for profit or non-profit business want to be seen locally, nationally, or internationally? Do you want to keep your focus of social responsibility on "bucket carrying" or "pipeline creation?" Do you want to react when a generous supporter suggests they have real estate to donate? Or are you ready to be PROACTIVE in attracting these Legacy Listings that benefit causes, careers, communities, and companies?

Those are important questions to answer before discussing how to leverage and implement a Cause Marketing Campaign. For example, there is a BIG difference between the following two scenarios.

Scenario #1: Create a page on your website that says, "We now accept real estate gifts," and put an "oh, by the way" type of blurb on your newsletter. (And, no, you don't "accept" real estate, you benefit from the proceeds; but that's typical verbiage.)

Scenario #2: Making a **BIG DEAL** about it and dedicating the whole newsletter to the topic, and shooting a video with your CEO, executive director, founder, or person in charge of philanthropy who shares the enthusiasm you have about this!

We are not suggesting this be your only form of funding or outreach. However, we suggest your cause, community, and company take this as *seriously as you do.* YOU have con**trol over positioning this as "Oh by the way," or "OHH MY GOD, look at what we found and want to bring to your attention!"**

Positioning

Whether you update, upgrade, and upscale positioning yourself or have our expert charitable gifting of real estate-focused marketing team do it for you, we have intended to inspire you to understand the benefits of this. Visit www.theraoc.com/ book_for some examples of positioning that our team has created for other REAL Agents of Change.

Our "Legacy Launch-pad" program gives you access to templates, scripts, emails, social media posts, zoom backgrounds, business cards, branded marketing material, and presentations that we create for you, and you can do it yourself for others. This is all designed to help you position yourself in the charitable gifting of real estate revolution at any level you feel inspired to position yourself. Once you are positioned and have had others attend some of the presentations so they understand the concept, you can start looking for partners.

The REAL Agents of Change

Video/Audio #36 of the following Section at:
www.theraoc.com/book#recording36

Cause Marketing Campaign Explanation

34

Sample Cause Marketing Campaign

Let's implement this campaign for a foundation that funds many non-profits to show how this can work for you, them, and those we all serve. This kind of campaign could be done with any "sub-niches" or with ALL non-profits and causes.

Let's keep it simple and look at a Cause Marketing Campaign (CMC) that focuses on lead generation, Legacy Listings, and Leveraging "locally." Yet, others from around the country can participate from live streams. Keep in mind that the "Strategy" of WHO you want to talk to, WHAT you want to say, and HOW you want to say it all depends on the outcome or "payoffs" you want. Therefore, your campaigns can focus on any of the following and more.

- A National Day or Holiday
- Specific funding needs...building a new school or house
- November, the month of "Giving Tuesday"
- Conserving a piece of land that is at risk
- The overall education and awareness that charitable real estate gifting is an option

We will assume you want to meet and mingle with other human beings in a physical setting. If that is your preference, this can be modified, done online, or with social distancing in mind.

Partnering & Promoting

Promoting is a lot more fun, efficient, and effective when you are not doing all of it by yourself. We will even go so far as to say it is selfish to want to promote it by yourself. Why? Without partners, you cannot reach the masses or bring in LOTS of Legacy Listings to fund those you say you're here to serve. You are also not leveraging the benefits to other non-profits, for profits, Influencers, advisors, and fund-raisers who equally benefit from partnering with you. They may have a different "P1" and "P2", but if they want to increase their Resources, Relationships, and Revenue, charitable gifting of real estate and the Positioning, Partnering, and Promoting would serve them well.

Our invitation is to think of all the people you know in these categories and really think it through. How would being seen as socially responsible help them? What are their benefits of having a fun, engaging way to reach out to their 200 or 2,000 past clients? What would their non-profit do with the average $550,000 net proceeds of a real estate donation? How would the mortgage broker, banker, coffee shop owner, print shop, Realtor, CEO, fund-raiser, or "insert profession" benefit from this conversation? What doors will open from high-level conversations and human interaction during a Legacy Listing, and how do The REAL Agents of Change leverage them?

Side thought: *If you are having difficulty seeing how this builds Resources, Relationships, and Revenue, you are not ready to implement any of the strategies in this book. I've met people who just don't get it, and the struggle is real for them. We love you. We are grateful you've read this far, and we encourage you to reread it later as we are different people three and six months or a year into the future. This requires a truly abundant mindset and one who is experiencing life through the filter of,*

"How does this benefit others?"

vs.

"How does this benefit me?"

This campaign is only for those who have BIG VISION. It requires you to have faith and expect that people to be positive and want to be part of the solution at heart.

The REAL Agents of Change

deo/Audio #37 of the following Section at:
www.theraoc.com/book#recording37

Sample CMC, Cause Marketing Campaign

35

Sample CMC

A *Cause Marketing Campaign* is a campaign that markets businesses with a cause in mind. This sample campaign is being executed by "The Foundation" and will leverage: **National List a Legacy Listing Month!**

When you write YOUR book, you can shamelessly promote YOUR National Month! "National List a Legacy Listing Month" is in April and is exactly what it sounds like. It's a month we celebrate the charitable gifting of real estate and do so with Listing a Legacy Listing! Or at the very least, educating the public about how these Legacy Listings benefit Causes, Careers, Communities, and Companies.

Let's say this campaign is a collaboration that brings together the for profit and the non-profit communities to "Rally the Troops" to inform them that charitable gifting of real estate is an option and what this foundation is embracing. The campaign begins on February 1st.

- February 1st, the foundation schedules "The RAOC Revolution, Charitable Real Estate 101"
- The presentation is scheduled for February 15th to be held live and live-streamed
- The Foundation provides the physical location
- Three Emails announcing
  - "National List a Legacy Listing Month" and what that means to The Foundation
  - There is an event to support The Foundation

that is not a "fund-raiser" but an "Awareness Raiser"

- Details on how they can register to attend in person or live stream
- If The Foundation wants to sell tickets as a fund-raiser, they can. There are pros and cons.
- Three Social Media Posts
  - "National List a Legacy Listing Month" and what that means to The Foundation
  - There is an event to support The Foundation that is not a "fund-raiser" but an "Awareness Raiser"
  - Details on how they can register to attend in person or live stream
- Touch campaign to reach out to the "Top 10" in all the categories mentioned previously and any others that are appropriate for this foundation, mission, area, and campaign
- Because THIS Cause Marketing Campaign focuses on "National List a Legacy Listing Month," the real estate industry is even more important. Mortgage, Title, Appraisers, all "real estate groupies," and real estate agents. THE MORE, THE BETTER! Whole real estate companies, offices, and Top Producers will be interested in this.
- All Foundation Board members, fund-raisers, volunteers, and support people make this same list for themselves
- All these supporters send the emails and create social media posts
- All of them reach out personally to their Top 10 lists
- Keeping the "script," invitation, and conversation

simple, short, enthusiastic, and WITHOUT lots of explaining. Remember, confused people do nothing. Just invite them to support The Foundation with their attendance.

- The ONLY "Yes" they are looking for is a "YES! I'd love to learn more! Thank you for the invite!"
- The presentation is done and recorded.
- Co-Branded with the C.C.R.E.S. involved and the non-profit hosting the presentation.
- Presentation is HIGH ENERGY, fun, engaging, and completely focused on information and education. There is NO SELLING. PERIOD.
- Remember, one of the best things about what The RAOC is helping with is that there is no need to sell or convince anyone of anything.
- This stage is the "Seed Planting" phase of providing options everyone involved did not know were available.
- Recording can be sent, but do not offer that as a substitute for being at the event live.
- Follow up with supporting material regarding CGRE
- Provide support material to those in attendance of the presentation who want to plant their seeds to find Legacy Listings to List during National List a Legacy Listing Month!
- Notice that the campaign starts long before the National List a Legacy Listing Month because, in this campaign, we want to raise awareness, plant

the seeds, and potentially "List a Legacy Listing" during that month.

NOTICE: EVERYONE who supports and serves this non-profit gets involved! Just like if they were planning a gala that took all year to plan and create. Only with this...**ALL they are doing is inviting their WARM markets to learn something they want to learn about. They are doing their contacts a favor with the invite.**

We know it may be a stretch for some people to believe. How could inviting people to this overview be doing them a favor? Because 99.9% of people have no idea about charitable gifts of real estate (yet). Millions of dollars will flow into this community. Gifting smarter with tax incentives will happen. Businesses and advisors will earn more money. The WIN-WIN-WIN of CGRE The RAOC way of "Position, Partner, & Promote" with TONS of Payoffs has begun!

Visit www.theraoc.com/listalegacy for more information about this recognized month and ways to leverage it in your market, marketing, and marketplace.

The REAL Agents of Change

Video/Audio #38 of the following Section at:
www.theraoc.com/book#recording38

The BIG Picture, First 3 P's

36

Let's look at the **BIG PICTURE** of this campaign from the perspective of The Foundation initiating it. Imagine this being your non-profit, real estate company, or whomever you are as a REAL Agent of Change going through the 7 P's from Purpose to Payoff ™.

P1: The Foundations Purpose
Their purpose is to support the "Right, Vetted" non-profits that already exist with the resources, relationships, and revenue they need to make their missions a reality. This foundation is full of savvy, successful, well-connected Influencers and business owners who see the vision. They want to tap into the "Wealth Bucket" called real estate, which is 43% of our wealth as a nation. Sure, they will take cash and are grateful for those who simply want to give them a check. However, they know that focusing on less than 3% of people's wealth is just not the best return on investment of their own time, talent, and treasure. They know that "cash" is not king and are taking a different approach to the funding they need to support the causes in their communities. They are starting in one community but with a national and international impact vision. Therefore, inviting their "Top 10" from all over in order to plant seeds far and wide.

P2: Purpose of Those They are Communicating with
They are capitalizing on "National List a Legacy Listing Month," which, by the way, you can too! Because they are capitalizing on a month that benefits all those in the real estate industry, it is a no-brainer to blast this invitation to the thousands who benefit

from more real estate transactions. Now because we are talking about charitable gifts of real estate, WAY MORE people than real estate professionals benefit from real estate. The marketing, emails, social media posts, and conversations to invite them to learn about "National List a Legacy Listing Month" can include verbiage about the following.

- "FULL Commissions" to List The Legacy Listing
- Make Money Making a Difference
- Real Estate for REAL Change
- Help our cause by helping your company List The Legacy Listings

P3: Presence

The presence of internal conversation The Foundation members are communicating from is different than if they were offering another fund-raiser, and another asks for cash or another event where the attendees are going in knowing they will leave with less money than they walked in with! No matter how worthy the cause or how wealthy the attendees are, there is a big difference between asking people to GIVE versus offering people A GIFT. Those who invite everyone, know they are giving the gift of options and opportunities.

- Options to "Give Smarter" and save money on their taxes
- Options for the non-profits to "Receive Smarter" and six times their endowments
- Opportunities for the businesses to attract 87%
- Of the consumers who choose them over the competition when they help promote this campaign and show up as socially responsible
- Opportunities for the real estate agents to earn

full commissions, have a unique sales proposition, and a reason to reach out to all their current and past clients about something not salesey or icky, and benefit everyone they talk to in one way or another!

THIS kind of campaign becomes FUN and Exciting!

The REAL Agents of Change

Video/Audio #39 of the following Section at:
www.theraoc.com/book#recording39

The BIG Picture, Second 3 P's

37

P4, P5, and P6: Positioning, Partnering, & Promoting

Let's talk about all these together. The Foundation can do a "Pre-event event" with their TOP 10. What if they invited the non-profits they directly support, the real estate company owners they have known for twenty years, the mortgage, the title, the insurance companies, the bank executives, their favorite restaurant owners, golf pro, and jewelry store owners? What if they have an event before the February 15th event? They invite those they know on a first-name basis and their lifelong friendships. Inviting them to "Position" themselves as socially responsible, "Partner" with these Influencers, advisors, and fund-raisers in a campaign to "Promote" a way to support ALL Causes, ANY Communities, and THEIR Careers and Companies by simply educating their customers, clients, vendors, and the general public that there is a smarter way to give and receive FUNding? This handful of selected potential partners could be invited to an exclusive:

**"Make Money Making a Difference,
How to Leverage Charitable Real Estate to Fund
Your Causes, Companies, and Communities"**

This one is before February 1st, so these Influencers, advisors, and fund-raisers can make a good business decision for themselves. Then, once they see the untapped potential that is charitable gifting of real estate, imagine how broad of a reach (thousands of people) would be touched, moved, and inspired!

Instead of The Foundation doing all the promoting by

themselves, they would have partners promoting with them, sending the emails, social media posts, and making their own Top 10 lists. Not only because they love The Foundation and believe in it, but also because *they see what's in it for their cause, career, community, and company.*

P7: Leave a Legacy

Ultimately, can you see all the "Legacy Listings" that would be listed during National List a Legacy Listing Month! This year… next year…and for years to come! But, of course, all the months before and after April, too!

THIS, my friends, is how you resign from the proud "Bucket Carriers Club" and create a pipeline full of flowing fun—FUNding that leaves a legacy from Legacy Listings in this lifetime and for generations to come.

Key #4: Leverage

Leveraging can be accomplished in a variety of ways. It can involve just you, your non-profit, and your donor list. It could be doing Facebook live videos and other social media campaigns letting your followers know you can benefit from gifts of real estate. It can be getting interviewed on local tv or getting national exposure. There are as many ways to leverage Legacy Listings and charitable gifting of real estate as there are the 1.3M non-profits, the 2M real estate agents, and the millions of professionals who benefit from this business development. To strategize a Cause Marketing Campaign for your Cause, Community, or Company, contact cami@theraoc.com.

The REAL Agents of Change

Video/Audio #40 of the following Section at:
www.theraoc.com/book#recording40

The BIG Picture, Leaving a Legacy

38

Key #5: Leaving a Legacy

As you can see, there is a lot more to this "Leaving a Legacy" thing than just knowing what charitable gifting of real estate is. Are you beginning to understand how much of a WIN-WIN-WIN Charitable Gifting of Real Estate is for everyone?

Legacy by Definition:

- Something (such as property or money) that is received from someone who has died—often a substantial gift that needs to be properly managed
- Something transmitted by or received from an ancestor or predecessor or the past

As a REAL Agent of Change, our legacies do not need to wait until we have died. However, they are so substantial that they will need to be properly managed! And that is just the cash part. The REAL Legacy here is being transmitted from us as the ancestors who had Vision, TOOK ACTION, and started the new trend in how non-profits are funded through The RAOC Revolution. We are leaving a legacy for our children. Instead of begging friends and family members to buy a fundraising candy bar, we can help the children, animals, elderly, veterans, and our planet by performing noble tasks of volunteering, visiting senior centers, writing letters to our enlisted people overseas, or planting seagrass in the dunes. Our loved ones can do all these important, much-needed tasks because we shifted from "fundraising" to "FUN Raising," "Awareness Raising," and "FRIEND Raising."

Okay, I can hear the groans and feel the blood boiling from the "fund-raisers" out there whose job it is to raise funds and from the people who are social butterflies and love a good gala or golf tournament! One of the best times I ever had was at a "Meat Auction" hosted by drag queens to raise funds in Massachusetts!

We are not suggesting stopping all fund-raisers. We are simply saying that because you truly do need funds, how about adding the logo on the flyer of your next event that you can benefit from real estate gifts? How about you sprinkle in some educational "Awareness Raisers" so those who want to support your cause can make informed, educated decisions about what makes the most sense for them?

What if you could bring in SIX TIMES what you currently are by simply adding at the end of every fund-raiser call to the donors you already call, **"By the way, Mary, we have recently heard about how wonderful animal lovers like you appreciate the ability to learn how they can give smarter through gifts of real estate. We are hosting a zoom on Tuesday, and I know you would love to have an invite and be in the know about how it works."**

You can add these simple statements with confidence, excitement, and enthusiasm when you KNOW you have a real estate team whose got your back! Real Estate Companies all over the country are adding **"Charitable Real Estate Divisions C.R.E.D."**

C.R.E.D.-ability: Do you have YOUR C.R.E.D.-ability?
These are run by local Certified Charitable Real Estate Specialists C.C.R.E.S. who host these events in their backyards, conference rooms, and zooms. Progressive Community Foundations are

developing "C.R.E.D.-ability" for themselves by funding communities with real estate from all over the country —and in some cases, the world. They are learning that if it's local, mortgage-free, and easy, they can handle it. Yet they do not want to be limited in their ability to leave their legacy.

What is YOUR Legacy to the world? SERIOUSLY! We want to know! We invite you to join the Facebook group.
www.facebook.com/groups/therealagentsofchange

Post in the group what your legacy will be or already has begun to be. We are a Visionary, Forward-Thinking group of Trailblazers, Do-Gooders, Bushwackers, and Change Agents. We support a community culture of collaboration. We want to get to know you, celebrate you, honor you, and acknowledge you. After all, you've made it to the end of this book, and that took an open mind. So based on that, we like you already.

If you are a visionary non-profit ready to Leave a Legacy from Legacy Listings, let's put you in touch with real estate professionals and financial service providers who can support you. Whether they are already in our group and will love you when they meet you, or whether they are the army we create together from your current tribe and those who will find you from our marketing together.

When advisors can "Make Money" for themselves by "Making

a Difference" with you and for you, it is a beautiful community culture of collaboration. We can show you how to leverage it.

If you are an inquisitive property owner who had no idea you could Leave a Legacy right now, while you have the blessing of seeing the fruits of your life, we welcome you!

We know that 80% of you are simply BIG HEARTED, generous, heart-centered, philanthropic people who just feel good doing the right thing.

Maybe you are like Linda and didn't know you could be so generous from the "tenants, trash, and toilets" that have been weighing you down anyway. Maybe you are a high-net-worth individual with lots of property and lots of need for exit strategies that soften your tax blow. Either way, the beauty of Charitable Gifts of Real Estate is that no matter why the gifts are gifted, the non-profit world benefits, and for that, we are grateful you are here.

If you are a seasoned, professional advisor who has always been the one sitting on committees, running the fund-raisers, giving hefty donations from your pocket, carrying rolls of raffle tickets in your bag, and investing more time, talent, and treasure than anyone else in your marketplace, yet feeling like it's a never-ending battle to help another cause, another group, another event... WELCOME!

The REAL Agents of Change

Video/Audio #41 of the following Section at:
www.theraoc.com/book#recording41

Imagining a New World

39

Imagine the following Legacy, my new friend. It's a world where even the smallest non-profit can do big things with the funding they only dreamed of when cash was the only option. A world where the largest non-profits can do SIX TIMES the work they once did with SIX TIMES the funding they once had! It is a world where generous, loving, kind supporters of all these non-profits have options and opportunities to give smarter from their wealth bucket of real estate.

Can you see the smiles on their faces, just like Linda's? Instead of $25 a year, she was proudly giving $39,000. Can you imagine how she feels when postcards, mailers, and emails go out to thousands of supporters of that cause and sharing the story—HER story—to inform, encourage, inspire, and ignite new abilities to be a blessing for all those who read it?

Are You ready to be on TV?
Like millions of "For Sale" signs before, there are "For Sale" signs in front of houses, strip malls, raw land, and office buildings. However, now there's another sign next to it that says: **"100% of the proceeds from this property supports non-profits, including "Your Non-profits logo inserted."**

Oh, look! There is a big van with a satellite dish on top and bright, bold letters on the side that spell out your local news channel WMUR. There is a reporter with a microphone standing next to the real estate agent of this Legacy Listing, and the non-profit's Executive Director is there. The reporter asks, "Jessica Peterson of EXP Realty, "How did you learn to fund this non-profit with real estate? I hear there is $575,000 going to this fabulous non-profit from this. What did you call it? Legacy Listing?" Once Jessica's given her brilliant reply, the reporter turns to the Executive Director and asks, "What will your non-profit do with $575,000?"

You see, my new friend, this is a HOT TOPIC. It is a BOLD new designation. It is a paradigm shift in how non-profits are being funded.

Imagine the interview happening on a very busy road with hundreds of cars passing by, curious about this spectacle. And what about the viewing audience as it airs on TV? Thousands of non-profits in that marketplace will know to reach out to Jessica Peterson at jessica@luxourteam.com to help their non-profit. Next, thousands of property owners will learn they can consider this a viable option for their estate planning.

(Left to Right: Hallie Peilet, Jessica Peterson, Cami Baker)

"We at The Haven feel so grateful to be the featured non-profit in this insightful and helpful book. When Cami first came to me and told me about CGRE, and the endless possibilities, I was mind blown. I realized not many donors know this is an option for a seamless donation to their favorite organization, with several tax benefits included. I also realized many non-profits might think it's a 'hassle' to accept a gift of real estate. Thanks to Real Agents of Change and the Specialized Non-profit, that couldn't be further from the truth. They make the whole process, start to finish, as easy as possible. Between real estate agents, non-profits, and donors, it is a win-win-win to be involved in the gifting of this kind!"

Hallie Peilet Director of Mission Engagement
The Haven 4405 Desoto Road
Sarasota, FL 34235

This is why these are Legacy Listings. This is how your non-profit can be part of "The Awakening" and get funded by the millions, therefore Leaving Lasting Legacy through Legacy Listings. This is why real estate professionals want to be "Certified Charitable Real Estate Specialists C.C.R.E.S.," love being a Champion, and become a Legacy Listings Lister. This is how professional financial representatives can List and Liquidate Legacy Listings to add to their "Assets Under Management AUM." They can also be "Certified Charitable Real Estate Specialists C.C.R.E.S."

The REAL Agents of Change

Video/Audio #42 of the following Section at:
www.theraoc.com/book#recording42

I AM A Real Agent of Change Declaration

40

We remind you now to revisit this question, these bold statements, and this exclusive invitation:

Are YOU a REAL Agent of Change?

I Am a Real Agent of Change

A **REAL Agent of Change** takes a STAND for those we are called forth to serve and support.

We believe you can make excuses, or you can MAKE IT HAPPEN, but you CANNOT do both.

We are Go-Getters, Do-Gooders, Trailblazers, and Visionaries who know that Making Money and Making a Difference SHOULD go hand-in-hand.

A **REAL Agent of Change** is open to new ideas, eager to TAKE ACTION, and BOLDLY goes where others cannot even see.

We plant our flag, burn our bridge, and walk through the fire to RISE UP transformed.

We look for reasons why something WILL WORK, not why it won't.

When others ask, "Why bother?" a **REAL Agent of Change's** motto is: *"If it is a benefit to all, including myself, then I MUST do it!"*

We SERVE instead of Sell.

We COLLABORATE vs. Compete.

We understand that GIVING and RECEIVING are simultaneous.

We know the difference between a transaction and a TRANSFORMATION.

A **REAL Agent of Change** is INFLUENTIAL and uses this SUPERPOWER for GOOD!

We know that our ACTIONS, or lack thereof, have an IMPACT on our family, community, marketplace, and the world. We do not take this for granted.

We Inspire. We are Inspired. We are Inspiring.

We are an Inspiration for everyone we meet!

A **REAL Agent of Change** knows that we can DOUBLE PROFITABILITY for ourselves and all those with whom we partner.

We are Passionate, Purposeful, Playful, Pragmatic, Present, and Positioned as a Partner who PRO-MOTES, PROMOTES, PROMOTES the benefits of Charitable Real Estate, knowing our Causes, Careers, Companies, and Communities deserve a **WIN-WIN-WIN!**

You may think I am hopeless idealistic romantic, but I am not. I am a committed visionary revolutionist. I assure you, as enough of you catch the same vision and take a stand, we will unite communities across the nation and affect change throughout the world...because we are The REAL Agents of Change! People like YOU are stepping into RAOCSTARDOM every day. And for that, I am truly grateful.

By reading this book, you've already turned Key #1 and unlocked the door of knowledge. Will you turn Key #2 by sharing this book with someone you care about? It is that simple, my friends. The RAOC Revolution needs you. Will you answer the call?

~ The REAL Agent of Change AKA Cami C.E. Baker

The REAL Agents of Change

Video/Audio #43 of the following Section at:
www.theraoc.com/book#recording43

Quote by Danielle Cummings A.K.A. Donation Diva

THE REAL AGENT OF CHANGE!

FOUNDER
(AKA LADY LEGACY)

About Cami C.E. Baker

Friends, there's no way to properly introduce the one and only Cami C.E. Baker... The Mingle To Millions Maverick who has evolved into The REAL Agent of Change. For example, I could tell you that she has excelled in real estate, lead generation, hosting networking events, public speaking, and partnering for profits with non-profits for almost two decades. Racking up an incredible resume, whether as an HGTV House Hunter Veteran, Top 5% Realtor, and Author of the award-winning "Mingle to Millions" and Cause Marketing Campaign Strategist, to name a few. But she's also the epitome of classy, sassy, and brassy; and if you knew her at all, no matter whether you like her or not, you'd know she was destined to lead this revolution.

By definition, Cami is a leader, a revolutionist, a heart-centric do-gooder, and a trailblazer... SHE LIVES & BREATHES THE RAOC DECLARATION. The bottom line, her unique ability to see opportunity and create cash flow for her clients has led to the ultimate "Make Money Making a Difference" and WIN-WIN-WIN of a lifetime!

THIS IS WHAT SHE WAS MEANT TO DO... HER DESTINY... HER CALLING... SHE IS EQUIPPED TO MAKE A REAL DIFFERENCE ONCE AND FOR ALL!

SIREN FOR 'THE AWAKENING'

"The Awakening" has begun, and we've joined forces with the likes of Dr. Russell James to drive awareness that there is a better way to fund your causes... that leveraging not just real estate but all non-cash assets is not just a good way to Give More, but it's how to Give Smarter!

CHAMPION FOR ALL CAUSES
THE ANCESTORS OF TRUE & LASTING LEGACY.

Our unique contribution is in attracting altruistic, brilliant, visionary Influencers, donors, charities, Charitable Real Estate Specialists, and CHAMPIONS who share a passion for meeting the needs in our communities and the world by funding, in mass, the charities who are positioned to affect change. Then providing them the skills through the C.R.E.S. Certification is the business development element needed to successfully implement their knowledge around Charitable Gifting of Real Estate through training, strategy, and marketing. And, together, we're breaking the chains of lack-mentality, lack-funding, and at long last, bridging the gap between non-profits and their donors.

Do we have a hidden agenda? NO! No matter which cause(s) you want to champion. We want to see ALL of the 1.4 million (and counting) public charities receive the funding they need to make the difference in our communities and the world that is so desperately needed! Neither does it matter what your payoff is. We each have a reason that motivates us, and money should be a part of the equation. You should *make money making a difference!*

We believe: **Good people should have good things happen to them!**

And if you are reading these words here at the end of this book, whether you originally picked up the book because the title set you on fire or because you were angered by the implication that fundraising, while valiant, is a small-minded way of funding a cause... **YOU have the heart that is needed to make a real change, a true and lasting legacy. YOU are exactly who we want and who we need to have standing with us during this Revolution!**

WE ARE THE RAOC REVOLUTION!

As the "Robin" to Cami's "Batman"... the "Donation Diva" to "Lady Legacy"... and Co-Founder of The REAL Agents of Change, it is my honor to build this legacy, not only with Cami but, with each of you who help to champion our cause. From the bottom of my heart, I thank you for your support and for taking a stand with us!

~ Danielle Cummings
A.K.A Donation Diva

Danielle Cummings
CO-FOUNDER
(AKA DONATION DIVA)

Links Index

- www.theraoc.com/book#recording15
  The 7 P's from Purpose to Payoff
- www.theraoc.com/book#recording16
  Specialist vs. Champion
- www.theraoc.com/book#recording17
  First 3 P's
- www.theraoc.com/book#recording18
  Second 3 P's Positioning and Partnering
- www.theraoc.com/book#recording19
  Second 3 P's Continues with P6 Promoting
- www.theraoc.com/book#recording20
  The 7th P: The Payoff
- www.theraoc.com/book#recording21
  Ooohh...The Inspiration
- www.theraoc.com/book#recording22
  First Action Step
- www.theraoc.com/book#recording23
  WARM Market vs. COLD Market
- www.theraoc.com/book#recording24
  Your Top 10 Lists
- www.theraoc.com/book#recording25
  WHO, WHAT, and HOW...Let's Plant Seeds
- www.theraoc.com/book#recording26
  Simple Script
- www.theraoc.com/book#recording27
  The Legacy Launch-pad (™) Process
- www.theraoc.com/book#recording28
  Key #3 List and Liquidate, The Seed Analogy
- www.theraoc.com/book#recording29
  What is The Legacy Listing?
- www.theraoc.com/book#recording30
  The Two-Step Process

- www.theraoc.com/book#recording31
RAOC Testimony
- www.theraoc.com/book#recording32
The CGRE Road-map Explained
- www.theraoc.com/book#recording33
Key #4: Leverage
- www.theraoc.com/book#recording34
What IF?
- www.theraoc.com/book#recording35
Position, Partner, & Promote
- www.theraoc.com/book#recording36
Cause Marketing Campaign Explanation
- www.theraoc.com/book#recording37
Sample CMC, Cause Marketing Campaign
- www.theraoc.com/book#recording38
The BIG Picture, First 3 P's
- www.theraoc.com/book#recording39
The BIG Picture, Second 3 P's
- www.theraoc.com/book#recording40
The BIG Picture, Leaving a Legacy
- www.theraoc.com/book#recording41
Imagining a New World
- www.theraoc.com/book#recording42
I AM A Real Agent of Change Declaration
- www.theraoc.com/book#recording43
Quote by Danielle Cummings A.K.A. Donation Diva

All Other Links

ALL resources are found at **www.theraoc.com/bookresources**

- www.theraoc.com/vip
- www.theraoc.com/masterclass
- www.theraoc.com/donations
- www.theraoc.com/propertyevaluation
- www.theraoc.com/faqs#reports
- www.theraoc.com/listalegacy
- www.theraoc.com/book
- www.theraoc.com/bookresources
- www.theraoc.com/book#road-map
- www.theraoc.com/book#faqs
- www.theraoc.com/book#samples
- www.theraoc.com/book#interviews
- www.theraoc.com/book#101
- www.theraoc.com/book#m2m
- www.facebook.com/groups/therealagentsofchange

Made in United States
Orlando, FL
15 February 2024

43724057R00147